100 Years of Women's Basketball

Sandra Steen and Susan Steen

Twenty-First Century Books

Brookfield, Connecticut

In memory of our father, Thomas Cradit Steen,
who introduced us to the love of sports.

Acknowledgments:
To editors Laura Walsh, Lorrie Barrett, Amy Shields, and Kristen Bettcher for their suggestions.
To Nan Elrod, director of programs at the Women's Basketball Hall of Fame, for her input.
To the staff at the Naismith Memorial Basketball Hall of Fame for the use of their library.

Cover photographs courtesy of Naismith Memorial Basketball Hall of Fame and AP/Wide World Photos

Photographs courtesy of Naismith Memorial Basketball Hall of Fame: pp. 12, 15, 18, 19, 22, 27, 41, 45, 58, 64, 69, 70, 71, 80, 100; © Bettmann/Corbis: pp. 13, 30; Team Stewart: pp. 35, 36; Getty Images: pp. 37 (Hulton), 46 (Hulton), 49 (Hulton), 82 (Archive Photos); AP/Wide World Photos: pp. 55, 76, 120; Timepix: pp. 75 (© James Drake), 83 (© Patrick Murphy-Racey), 88 (© David E. Klutho), 89 (© Al Tielemans), 97 (© David E. Klutho), 103 (© Al Tielemans), 105 (© David E. Klutho), 116 (© John W. McDonough); Corbis: p. 91 (© Reuters NewMedia Inc.); NBA Entertainment: p. 113 (© Andrew Bernstein); Women's Basketball Hall of Fame: pp. 121 (Neil Studios/Neil & Elizabeth Crosby), 122 (Neil Studios/Neil & Elizabeth Crosby)

Library of Congress Cataloging-in-Publication Data
Steen, Sandra.
Take it to the hoop : 100 years of women's basketball / Sandra Steen
and Susan Steen.
p. cm.
Summary: Traces the development of women's basketball, from its
beginning in the 1890s through the formation of the Women's National
Basketball Association in 1997.
Includes bibliographical references (p.   ) and index.
ISBN 0-7613-2470-4 (lib. bdg.)
1. Basketball for women--United States--History--Juvenile literature.
2. Basketball players--United States--Biography. 3. Women basketball
players--United States--Biography. [1. Basketball for women--History.]
I. Steen, Susan. II. Title.
GV886 .S78 2003   796.323'082--dc21
2002011988
Published by Twenty-First Century Books
A Division of The Millbrook Press, Inc.
2 Old New Milford Road
Brookfield, Connecticut 06804
www.millbrookpress.com

100 Years of Women's Basketball

Contents

Introduction: Welcome to the Ball

The Boomers' sneakers squeak as they hustle for the ball. Trina grabs the **rebound** and throws an **outlet pass** to her teammate, starting a **three-on-one fast break**. The lone Cheetah defender fails to **block**. A third Boomer scores an easy **bucket**.

Fans stomp their feet and whistle.

The ball goes to the **baseline** for a throw in. The Cheetah **point guard** signals a play. She **dishes** the ball to her teammate, who bounce passes it back to her.

The crowd yells, "**De-fense**! De-fense!"

The point guard passes to another teammate, who shoots an **airball**. A Boomer rebounds and dribbles to the Cheetah's basket. She throws a chest pass to Trina, who gets **double-teamed**.

Trina looks for an opening and passes the ball to another Boomer. The Boomer makes a **pump fake** and shoots a blank. Trina leaps high and grabs the rebound. She throws it out of the **paint** to another Boomer, who **drives** against a Cheetah.

"**Shake and bake**," a fan yells.

After an attempted steal, the loose ball rolls across court. Trina dives for it.

The crowd jumps to its feet. "Boomers! Boomers!"

Trina pivots and **knocks one down from behind the arc**.

The crowd roars. The buzzer blares. Halftime. The Boomers lead, 44–41.

This fictional game shows how active women's basketball is today. But games weren't always like this. Women's basketball started more than a hundred years ago, and since then it has traveled a long, hard road. Women have gone from playing in long dresses, to winning Olympic gold medals, to competing on professional teams, and finally to being inducted into the Women's Basketball Hall of Fame.

Definitions of Some Basketball Terms

airball: shot that misses both hoop and backboard

baseline: the boundary line under each basket

blank: missed shot

block: defensive play to stop the ball from going into the basket

bucket: basket

defense: team without the ball; defends its basket and tries to prevent the other team from scoring

dish: pass the ball

double team: two defensive players guarding an offensive player

drive: dribble quickly toward the opposing team's basket

knock one down from behind the arc: make a shot worth three points from behind the three-point line, 19 feet 8 inches from the basket

outlet pass: long pass after a rebound to start a fast break

paint: colored rectangles at either end of the court under the baskets; the free throw lane

point guard: player who brings the ball up the court and signals teammates for the play

pump fake: player with the ball pretends to shoot, hoping to get the person guarding her to jump up to block; when the defender comes down, the player with the ball attempts to make a clean shot

rebound: missed shot that is grabbed by any player

shake and bake: all kinds of fancy faking moves, including direction, passing, and shooting fakes

three-on-one fast break: the ball is passed to three different offensive players; the last one shoots a basket before a defense player can stop her

General Rules of Basketball

- A team consists of five players: two guards, two forwards, and a center.
- The ball can be passed, thrown, or dribbled across the court to the basket or goal.
- Field goals inside a three-point line are worth two points. Behind this line, they're worth three points.
- A personal foul occurs when a player pushes, holds, charges, or hits an opponent who is shooting the ball.
- When a player is fouled while shooting and makes the basket, she gets one free throw. If she missed her shot, she gets two free throws.
- Length of the game and time-outs vary depending on the level of play: high school, college, professional, or international.

Positions

- A forward plays nearest the basket (from the baseline to the free throw line), rebounds the ball, and gets close to the basket to make shots.
- A center is usually the tallest player and best rebounder.
- A guard plays farther away from the basket, is a good dribbler and passer, and directs the plays.
- The team with the ball plays offense, and their goal is to shoot baskets and score.
- The team without the ball plays defense and tries to prevent the other team from scoring or retaining possession of the ball.

Chapter 1

The Beginning of Women's Basketball: No Men Allowed

On March 21, 1893, Senda Berenson, the physical education director at Smith College in Northampton, Massachusetts, posted a note on the gymnasium door:

> **Notice:**
>
> **Gentlemen**
>
> **are not allowed**
>
> **in the gymnasium**
>
> **during basket ball games.**
>
> **— S. Berenson**

Two groups of women stood around the gym. They wore dark, below-the-knee baggy pants called bloomers, long-sleeved blouses, and long, thick stockings. The gym windows were covered because men were not allowed to watch women play the new game called "basket ball."

Inventor of the Game

Back in December, 1891, male students at the Young Men's Christian Association (YMCA) College in Springfield, Massachusetts, complained about their winter physical education classes. Tumbling, marching, and exercising bored them. Dr. Luther Gulick, Dean of Physical Education, and his faculty discussed the students' frustrations. Gulick suggested they create an indoor game of skill that promoted good sportsmanship. Most of the teachers tried, but failed.

The students at the YMCA College in Springfield, Massachusetts, were bored of the traditional indoor exercises in physical education classes during the winter. This gym is where the idea for a brand-new sport was conceived.

One instructor, James Naismith, realized that the walls of the gym limited the type of play suitable for an indoor game. He felt it would be dangerous for players to use a stick or bat indoors. Naismith created a game that would be played with a soccer ball that students could throw to each other. To eliminate roughness, he banned tackling, kicking, dribbling, and running with the ball. Naismith listed 13 rules. He described the officials' duties and the fouls or consequences when players broke the rules.

To score a point, a player would toss the ball into a box. Naismith decided to raise the box off the floor because that would prevent either team from hovering over the box. He figured students would have a better chance to make points if the box was raised above their heads.

James Naismith invented the game of basket ball. Here, he carries the original ball and peach basket used in his new sport.

Before his noon class on December 21, 1893, Naismith asked Pop Stebbins, the custodian, to bring him two boxes. Instead Pop returned with two peach baskets. Naismith attached the baskets to the railing on the bottom of the balcony, which was 10 feet off the ground, at each end of the gym.

When the class arrived, Naismith divided his 18 students into two teams. To start the game, he threw the ball up between two opposing players. Each tried to bat the ball to a teammate. Once the ball was in play, teammates passed the ball back and forth. William Chase tossed the ball 25 feet and made a basket. Then someone perched on a ladder, removed the ball, and threw it onto the court. Chase made the only point of the game.

Naismith's new game went unnamed for a short time. One student, Frank Mahan, suggested the name Naismith Ball, but the inventor disagreed. Naismith thought that since the sport used a basket and a ball, the game should be called basket ball. By 1921 "basket ball" would become one word.

About a month later several women teachers from nearby Buckingham Grade School passed by the YMCA College during their lunch break. They heard lots of shouting coming from the gym and decided to investigate. The women went inside and saw men

Duck on the Rock

As a child, James Naismith played the game "duck on the rock." One player put a stone, "the duck," on a boulder. Then other players tried to knock it off with their stones. Perhaps Naismith thought about this game when he created basket ball.

tossing a soccer ball. They thought it looked like fun and asked Naismith how to play. He agreed to teach them. Soon after, the women teachers formed a team.

Senda Berenson

At nearby Smith College for women, physical education director Senda Berenson thought basket ball would be beneficial for her students. She had read about Naismith's game in the January 1892 YMCA College newspaper, *The Triangle*. In those days, most people considered this kind of game not socially appropriate or physically possible for women. Berenson thought playing by men's rules might be too strenuous and "unladylike." She adapted the men's rules to suit women. Berenson encouraged teamwork and

Senda Berenson, in the long dress, starts up a game of basket ball with the students of Smith College in Northampton, Massachusetts, where women played the first public basket ball game in March 1893.

discouraged roughness. She believed in the total mental, spiritual, and physical well-being of her students.

Berenson's students played the three-court game. Instead of running up and down the whole court, each woman was assigned to stay in one of three sections of the court. At first Berenson allowed from five to ten players on a team, depending on the size of the court. She did not allow her students to hold the ball for more than three seconds. A player could either toss or bounce the ball to a teammate, or dribble it not more than three times. The rules permitted a guard to raise her arms vertically over her head only to stop a forward from shooting. A guard could not touch the ball or the player. The game moved slowly. Most of the time the women stood still and waited to play.

Players made baskets from a stiff pose with a two-handed chest shot. These were worth one point. For free throws, which became known as "granny" shots, girls held the ball between their bent knees with two hands and lofted it toward the basket. A free throw was worth three points. After each basket, the teams returned to the center of the court, where an official tossed the ball up between two opposing players.

More Schools Create Teams

Before long, other schools and Young Women's Christian Associations (YWCAs) heard or read about basket ball. On the West Coast, the University of California (UC) Berkeley and Miss Head's School, a private girls' preparatory school, played the first interinstitutional women's basket ball game on November 18, 1892. At the start of the game each team of nine lined up at opposite ends of the court. As soon as the official tossed the ball into the center, the women scrambled for the ball. Miss Head's team won 6–5. A reporter for the *Berkeley Daily Advocate*, who knew little about this new game, called it "feminine football."

Women in Dubuque, Iowa, played their first basket ball games at the YMCA in 1893. At Iowa State College in Ames women formed teams with names like the Kickapoos and the Tadpoles. One team called themselves the No Eyes, because none of the women had the letter "i" in her name.

Frail Females

In the 1890s many doctors believed that because of their smaller bones and hearts, women should not play team sports. They feared that women might faint and need to be revived with smelling salts. Some doctors thought women might become fatigued and catch diseases.

A professor of physical education at Bryn Mawr College in Pennsylvania, Alice Bertha Foster, felt that women should have a complete physical examination before playing basket ball. If they passed the exam, they could play. Foster stressed that careful refereeing would limit injuries. She supported doctors' recommendations that women could not play during the first three days of their menstrual periods. Senda Berenson agreed. To prevent fatigue, Foster thought that women should not play for more than 30 minutes per game and not more than twice a week.

People in the South also believed that strenuous exercise was not healthy or socially acceptable for women. Parents raised their daughters to be quiet, gentle, and ladylike—not competitive. For example, students at Sophie Newcomb College, the women's branch of Tulane University, in New Orleans, Louisiana, came to school in carriages. They attended classes while their nannies waited outside.

Sophie Newcomb College required women to wear bloomers during physical education classes. Bloomers looked like men's trousers. They were made of wool cloth that billowed from the waist to the ankle, covered each leg, and were worn beneath a shorter skirt, allowing for freedom of movement.

First Balls and Baskets

When teams first played basket ball, they used a soccer ball. Players disliked these balls because they were small and difficult to bounce. A larger ball replaced the soccer ball. These basket balls were handmade.

In 1894, Overman Wheel Company, a bicycle manufacturer, designed a basket ball that measured from 30 to 32 inches and weighed from 18 to 20 ounces. It had a rubber bladder inside, a layer of canvas lining for shape and support, and leather panels stitched around the outside. The bladder was tightly inflated, and the ball was laced closed. When the laces hit the floor, the ball hopped any which way. After several games, it turned lumpy and had to be reinflated. But if the bladder needed repair, it could be removed easily from the ball by unlacing the leather cover. In 1899, A.G. Spalding & Brothers manufactured similar balls and stamped them with the words "OFFICIAL BASKET BALL."

The methods of retrieving the balls from the peach baskets differed from place to place. One method was to drill a

small hole in the bottom of the basket. Then someone poked a stick through the hole, pushing the ball out of the basket. Later, to speed up the game, the bottoms of the baskets were removed. Metal hoops with closed net bags replaced the peach baskets in 1893. After the ball went through the hoop, officials pulled a cord or chain to raise the net, forcing the ball to roll over the top of the hoop and drop to the floor.

That year baskets were fastened to wooden backboards. For a while, wire screens replaced these backboards. The screens prevented people in a balcony from pushing the ball into the basket. After repeated contact with the ball, the wire screens began to sag, and by 1895 the official backboard was wooden.

The Newcomb students refused to wear bloomers in class. They thought bloomers were too outlandish. Instead, they came dressed in hats, gloves, heels, and long bustled dresses with high necks and tight corsets! It wasn't until 1902 that Newcomb women accepted wearing bloomers during physical education classes.

Clara Baer

When Clara Baer, director of physical education at Newcomb, heard about basket ball, she wrote to James Naismith requesting information. Naismith sent her the rules and a diagram of a court with player positions. Baer looked at the sections on the diagram where the players stood. She thought that the players were supposed to stay in those sections for the entire game. Baer didn't realize that players were allowed to move around the whole court. When her students played, they had to stay in their assigned sections. This made the game move slowly.

Parents and doctors of the students at Newcomb complained that Baer's basket ball was too strenuous and rough. Baer considered their complaints and modified Naismith's rules in January 1894. Some of her new rules included:

- Changing the court size, depending on the number of players.
- Dividing the court into eight or eleven sections, depending on how many students played. This limited running space but encouraged passing the ball.
- Allowing players six seconds to attempt a goal without interference. (Later it was changed to four seconds.)
- Banning dribbling and guarding an opponent.
- Calling fouls if a player talked or yelled during a game.
- Changing baskets. Each time a team scored, they were not allowed to score in that same basket. Players on both teams stayed in their areas, but had to change from being offensive players to defensive players.

Baer mailed Naismith her rules. When he saw Baer's major changes, Naismith suggested she give her game a different name. In 1895, Baer published her rules under the name Basquette.

Follow These Rules

The first recorded intercollegiate women's basket ball game took place on April 4, 1896. Stanford University played against UC Berkeley. Five hundred female spectators cheered them on. Men were not allowed to watch the game. At one point when two men came in to fix the basket, the UC women supposedly screamed and hid in a corner. The teams played two 22-minute halves. Stanford won 2–1.

The University of Washington competed against Ellensburg Normal School on April 22, 1896. However, there were problems with the rules. Each team brought a different-size ball. Washington owned a standard-size Victor ball. It measured larger in circumference than Ellensburg's ball. Officials discussed the problem and decided to use the Victor ball.

During the game, another problem arose over stealing the ball. The Washington team's rules allowed "snatching" or stealing, but the Ellensburg team's rules didn't. A reporter for the *Ellensburg Capital* called the game unfair and felt that the rules needed to be agreed upon before a game started. Washington had won 6–3.

The rules were addressed during the 1899 Physical Training Conference in Springfield, Massachusetts. A committee suggested these modifications to standardize rules for women:

- No stealing the ball.
- No holding the ball for more than three seconds.
- No bouncing the ball more than three consecutive times.
- Divide the court into three equal areas.

Senda Berenson, known as the "Mother of Women's Basketball," pioneered the development of the game for women. Her modified rules remained in use for 75 years.

- Personal foul given if a player leaves her assigned area.

- Minimum of six players; maximum of nine.

- Encourage teamwork. Discourage players from dominating the ball.

Senda Berenson edited these guidelines, which were later published by the American Sports Publishing Company in 1901, along with basket ball articles for women and pictures of teams. Berenson became the first female editor of a sports publication. For 16 years she edited *Spalding's Basket Ball for Women*, which contained the official updated women's rules. Berenson became known as the "Mother of Women's Basketball."

Popularity Grows

In the late 1890s the College Heights Orange Association, near Los Angeles, California, used an image of a Pomona College woman basket ball player on the label of their navel oranges. They called their oranges basket balls. This may have been one of the first commercial advertisements for women's basket ball.

When women's basket ball games were played outdoors, men watched. But for indoor games the "no men allowed" rule continued. A San Francisco newspaper in 1899 reported that eight high school boys wearing dresses, gloves, stockings, and thick veils boldly attended a women's game played between Berkeley and Stockton High.

During school breaks male and female basket ball players returned home raving about the game, which they taught their younger brothers and sisters. One of James Naismith's students from Japan returned to his country and taught the game to his peers. By the end of the 1890s the game of basket ball had spread around the world.

Chapter 2

What Are the Rules?

At the turn of the twentieth century, three sisters from Pasadena, California, gained notoriety playing high school basket ball. The Pasadena High team had five players. Violet Sutton played center and her sisters May and Florence both played forward. The team went undefeated for two years. In 1902 they lost one game when an opposing team made a goal five seconds after the end of the game. In those days the rules were loose.

The following year the two oldest Sutton sisters graduated. Perhaps due to Pasadena's winning record, 33 girls tried out for the basket ball team in 1903. Each hopeful girl paid ten cents a month to practice twice a week before the tryouts. May Sutton made the team again. That same year five high school and three college teams from the area formed a league called the Girls Basket Ball League of Southern California. In this league high schools and colleges competed against each other. Pasadena High won the league's first championship.

In 1905 the *Los Angeles Times* printed articles about the rough games played in Los Angeles County between girls' basket ball teams. Some players pulled their opponents' hair. Shoving and sliding occurred all over the court. Complaints were cited about officials calling too many fouls. The officials seemed to favor certain teams. These tactics forced the Executive Board of the County League to make rule changes. One recommendation was to use officials who had no connection with any of the schools.

Rule Changes

Spalding published revised rules for women's basket ball in 1903. Instead of 20-minute halves, they became 15 minutes. In the past, players were allowed to dive for balls that went out-of-bounds. In some cases they raced down stairways and into bleachers, sometimes injuring themselves or spectators. If the ball landed in a balcony, fans scrambled after it. For safety reasons a new rule for an out-of-bounds ball was made. The team that caused the ball to go out-of-bounds lost possession of it.

By 1906 the rule book changed the number of players per team to a minimum of five instead of six. It added the five-second out-of-bounds rule, which meant a player had five seconds to throw the ball into play. And when a player committed a foul, the opposing team earned a free shot worth one point.

More foul descriptions and rules were added to the list in 1908:

- A player had to release the ball within three seconds or receive a foul.
- Two players could not guard an opponent who was shooting.
- A foul would be called if a player placed her hand on the ball when it was in an opponent's possession.
- If a player stepped over a boundary line, she was given a foul.
- A team earned one point if their opponents fouled three times. (In the past, a team had been awarded one point every time an opponent fouled.)
- If a player committed three fouls, she was warned. After a fourth foul, that player sat on the bench for the rest of the game.
- The bounce pass was eliminated.

Discussions about women's basket ball rules always focused on women's health, poise, and emotions. It seemed that some rules changed every year. Dribbling was constantly an issue. In men's rules the players could dribble all over the court. This created "star" players who hogged the ball. The women's rules committee thought this

Hoops and Backboards Continue to Change...

Different kinds of baskets continued to evolve. Some hoops had closed leather nets attached, because they were more durable than ones made of cord. Then in 1918 the open net was officially allowed, which put the ball back into play much sooner.

The backboard was usually suspended from the ceiling so that the space under the basket was clear of obstructions. It was wooden and painted white to provide a better view of the basket. In 1909 glass backboards became popular so that spectators' views would not be blocked. Some gyms had a scoreboard, which was considered an accessory, not an essential.

would be unladylike and banned dribbling altogether in 1910. Then in 1913, to speed up the game, knee-high dribbling was reinstated.

Sometimes, the woman who played center was allowed to run the whole court, but not allowed to shoot a basket. Then by 1917, if the center was allowed to play full court, she could shoot for baskets. The following year this rule was reversed.

There were no time-outs or substitutions in 1916. If a coach offered tips from the sideline, a foul was called. It was thought that if coaches talked to players, the players might get upset. By 1917 the number of fouls a player could commit before she was benched was increased to five. In 1918 a fouled player had to take the ball out-of-bounds instead of shooting a free throw. In addition, the bounce pass and limited use of substitutes were allowed.

Between 1919 and 1938 minimal rule changes occurred in the United States. Those changes had to do with scoring, substitutions, and time. For example, the points for the overhead and two-hand underhand throws changed from two points to one.

Substitution rules changed from allowing a player one re-entry per game to two re-entries per game. The minimum number of players on a team changed from five back to six.

The games formerly had two 15-minute halves with a 10-minute halftime. The length of the game changed to 8-minute quarters with a 10-minute halftime. The time limit between the first and second quarters and the third and fourth quarters changed to two minutes, with no coaching. The length of time-outs increased from two minutes to five minutes, then changed back to two minutes. The number of time-outs decreased from three to two. Time-out changes were based on the belief that the rest period reduced strain on the heart and prevented exhaustion.

This depiction of female basket ball players from Princeton University in New Jersey shows the typical bloomer-type uniforms worn by women throughout the beginning of the 1900s.

Uniforms

The rule system also included clothing. Players suited up in "costumes" or uniforms that were fashionable at the time. Most players wore knickers-style bloomers that gathered just below the knee and sport shirts in their school colors. Coaches insisted that players arrive at practice and

Edmonton Commercial Grads

In Edmonton, Alberta, Canada, Coach John Percy Page started a team called the Edmonton Commercial Grads in 1915. All but two of the women players had graduated from McDougal Commercial High School. Most were teachers and stenographers. Coach Page stressed that Grads should act like ladies first and basket ball players second.

With no gym available, the Grads played home games outdoors. Their hard work paid off. This pioneer team won 147 games in a row. From 1915 to 1940 the Grads won 14 Canadian championships.

In 1923 the Grads entered the first International Underwood Trophy competition, sponsored by a typewriter company. Their opponents, the world champion Cleveland Favorite Knits, suited up in their short shorts and tight jerseys. The Grads, dressed in bloomers and long stockings, beat the Knits in two straight games.

The Grads also traveled to the United States. In March 1926 they lost to Cleveland's Newman-Stern team during the final game of a four-game championship series. Looking for more competitions, the Grads became barnstormers, playing games anywhere they could, including Olympic exhibitions. While playing in Europe, they won 24 straight games. In Paris, the Grads beat the Linettes 53–14. Catholic clergymen were offended by women competing in public sports and criticized the Grads' uniforms.

The number of players leaving and new players joining the Grads were few. In its 25 years of existence the team membership totaled only 38 women. If a Grad got married, she had to quit the team. The team dissolved in 1940, with a total of 502 wins and 20 losses. Throughout their reign, the Grads were never paid.

games in freshly laundered uniforms. During rest periods, players could wear sweaters or cotton or wool sweatshirts.

Women often wore long stockings held up with tight elastic garters that interfered with blood circulation. To prevent blisters on their feet some players wore thin socks under other short woolen socks. Sometimes players also wore kneepads for protection. Canvas-top shoes with soles made of crepe, a textured rubber, were recommended for footwear. These kinds of shoes, the forerunner of today's sneakers, cushioned the feet and reduced fatigue.

Not Ladylike

In the early 1920s some educators, physicians, and members of the general public criticized women's organized sports. They felt women's sports were becoming too competitive, which they considered unladylike. They frowned upon women earning expensive trophies and valuable prizes. They also didn't approve of women being exploited by companies who used players to help them sell their products. They thought newspapers and radio broadcasts promoted "star" players rather than teamwork.

On the other hand, some educators complained that men got first choice and more use of the gyms. They were unhappy that women had to practice with poor-quality equipment and receive poor training. Male coaches trained most women, but physicians thought women should have female coaches. They felt women would be more comfortable discussing personal physical problems with a female coach.

In 1923 female physical education teachers voiced their concerns to the Women's Division of the National Amateur Athletic Federation (NAAF). This federation, organized in 1922, promoted physical fitness for all Americans. Lou Henry Hoover, future First Lady to President Herbert Hoover, chaired the first National Conference on Athletics and Physical Education for NAAF, held in Washington, D.C., in 1923. Hoover was the only female officer of NAAF. She agreed with the current protests concerning women's athletics.

Her committee offered many resolutions. Among them were:

- Female athletes should not be exploited by businesses.

- Women should play sports for fun and education rather than for winning.

- Women should focus on good sportsmanship rather than making and breaking records.

- Women should complete a medical examination before participating in an event.

- Female coaches should be hired.

- Women should gain emotional rewards rather than monetary awards from sports.

- Women should not compete in the Olympics or on interscholastic teams.

The National Association of Secondary School Principals (NASSP) supported NAAF resolutions. In 1925 the NASSP decided to eliminate varsity teams and state competitions. At that time 37 states competed in basketball championship tournaments, and 21 of them chose to drop their tournaments. The opposing 16 states thought some of the NAAF resolutions restricted the game and chose to continue with women's basketball tournaments.

Lou Henry Hoover, wife of President Herbert Hoover, was the only female officer of the National Amateur Athletic Federation in 1923. The committee offered many suggestions on the way women's athletics should be played. These resolutions were contrary to the way men's sports were played at the time.

Cookies and Milk

Some critics of women's sports wrote articles with titles like "Are Athletics Making Girls Masculine?" and "Sweet Things Have Scrap." To avoid the unladylike image, physical education teachers made efforts to connect basketball with social events. Early on these activities became known as "Cookies and Milk" events. The idea probably started with Senda Berenson, who used to serve snacks or plan elaborate dinners after the games.

Amateur Athletic Union to the Rescue

Another organization, the Amateur Athletic Union (AAU), opposed the NAAF resolutions. Founded in 1888 by a group of sports clubs, the AAU had only been sponsoring programs for men. In 1923 they admitted women's programs.

The AAU supported women's competitions. They wanted to profit from women's sports events by charging entry fees. The AAU sponsored the first National Women's Basketball Championship in 1926 in Pasadena, California, using men's rules. By 1929, the AAU championship became an annual event. The AAU was the only group keeping women's basketball alive.

Chapter 3

Queens of the Court

Girls' high school basketball was alive and well in various states from 1920 to 1940. Tournaments in Florida received plenty of newspaper coverage. The Texas girls' teams got strong news coverage, too. At times the Texas girls' games had more fans than the boys'.

Meanwhile, Oklahoma had Bertha Teague. She coached teams from 1927 to 1969 at Byng High School in Ada. Teague emphasized good physical conditioning, learning the fundamental skills, and making players believe in themselves. From 1936 to 1939 her Lady Pirates couldn't be stopped. They won 98 games in a row. Teague held the record for the most wins nationwide by a girls' coach at the high school level until 1991. Her teams took eight state titles.

Welcome to Iowa

Perhaps no state was as enthusiastic about girls' basketball as Iowa. Iowa girls were hooked. They played anywhere and everywhere.

Hot Air and Fancy Footwork

In the early 1900s some schools had wood-burning stoves or heaters in the center of their gym. A metal sheet was placed around the wood-burning stoves so the players wouldn't get burned. After the stove cooled, a mattress was wrapped around it for protection. At Hiteman School in Iowa, the hot air register blew out gusts of scorching heat from the floor. When the boys and girls played basketball, they developed fancy footwork to avoid the register. Anyone who fell onto the grate would get a waffle burn.

One high school in Iowa had an enrollment of 20 girls, and 15 of them played on the basketball teams. If there wasn't a gym, they played in church or school basements, above stores, in opera houses, and sometimes above a saloon.

On July 4, 1904, in Alta Vista, Iowa, one team played an exhibition game on a field where the grass had been burned off to make a court. After the game, the girls were covered with black soot.

In 1925 about 250 members of the Iowa High School Athletic Association (IHSAA) voted to stop sponsoring basketball tournaments for girls. They thought tournaments were too strenuous for them. But 25 male school superintendents, teachers, and coaches protested. They formed a new organization, the Iowa Girls High School Athletic Union (IGHSAU). Because of the union's commitment, Iowa girls' basketball tournaments survived.

Most of the IGHSAU educators worked at small rural schools where girls' basketball was a way of life. Since farm girls completed laborious chores every day, playing basketball was not strenuous for them. Some of these rural high school girls' teams had won state championships. The members of IGHSAU agreed that tournaments gave girls a chance to travel, meet people, and to develop discipline, self-confidence, and teamwork. With the support of the *Des Moines Register* and *Tribune* newspapers, the girls continued to find sponsors and schedule tournaments for their teams.

In 1926, 16-year-old Irene Silka, a Maynard High School player in Iowa, scored 110 points in a game against Hawkeye High. Maynard won the game, 127–13. Silka's record stands as the single highest scoring total in three-court basketball. She rarely stood still and could shoot baskets from all angles. During her junior and senior years, Silka averaged 33 points per game, and out of those 51 games, she was charged with only 15 personal fouls. In three seasons Silka made a total of 1,707 points!

Parade of Champions

A trip to Des Moines to play in the March state finals tournament was a luxury for rural Iowa girls. Teams asked businesses to donate money for their trips. Some girls had never stayed in a hotel before. Fans booked hotel rooms and bought tickets several months in advance. Profits from ticket sales paid for the operation of Iowa's state sports programs for girls.

Starting in the 1940s, the final night of the Iowa tournament was broadcast on television with a Parade of Champions. The parade included the champions of other girls' sports like softball, volleyball, track, and swimming. After the championship basketball game, trophies and flowers were awarded to the winners. Winning coaches took home a traditional red jacket. The all-tournament team was announced, as well as four or five players to be inducted into the Iowa Girls Basketball Hall of Fame.

The day after the tournament the champions ate breakfast with the governor and attended church. Afterward, they toured the state house. From there they took a bus ride home, and fans joined them in a car caravan. Their school honored them with a ceremony. Magazine reporters interviewed and photographed the girls. One reporter, Rod H. Chisholm, who wrote a syndicated sports column for 16 Iowa newspapers, called Iowa girls' basketball players the "Queens of the Court."

From Hats to Shoes

Over the years the style of girls' uniforms changed in Iowa and throughout the country. In the early 1920s some teams paid dressmakers to sew blouses with large collars and below-the-knee bloomers that took 4 yards of material for each leg. The uniform cost $1.50.

A.G. Spalding & Bros. advertised blue serge gymnastic suits for $4.50. Brilliantine uniforms, made from a glossy fabric, cost $6.00. Some teams wore middies

Middies

Spalding Middies possess a style and smartness that distinguishes them wherever observed. They have been designed and improved, from year to year, to coincide with the ideas of the modern school and college girl.

MODEL 11F

No. 00.	Unbleached Jean	$1.50
No. 3.	Chambray	2.00
No. 14.	Jean	1.50
No. 6.	Everfast Poplin	3.00
No. 7.	Everfast Suiting	2.75
No. 8L.	Lightweight Khaki	1.75
No. 18.	Kindergarten Cloth	2.00

MODEL 53

No. 00.	Unbleached drill	$1.50
No. 14.	Jean. White only	1.50
No. 6.	Poplin. Colors	3.00
No. 7.	Everfast suiting	2.75

Bloomers

OUR STANDARD MODEL 21

Spalding Bloomers have been considered for years the standard for gymnasium and athletic work. Our Model No. 21, developed by the most expert designers of athletic clothing in the country, is in use in hundreds of schools and colleges throughout the United States.

MODEL 21 is made in the following materials:

No. 2.	Jean. White only	$3.50
No. 3.	Chambray	3.50
No. 4.	Monks' Cloth. Black only	3.00
No. 6.	Poplin	5.75
No. 7.	Everfast Suiting	4.50
No. 8.	Khaki	3.50
No. 8L.	Khaki. Lightweight.	3.00
No. 18.	Kindergarten cloth	$3.50
No. 30.	Serge. All wool storm serge	5.50
No. 33.	Serge. (All wool)	8.50

This advertisement from Spalding shows the different possibilities and prices for women's athletic wear of the time. Notice they are marketing these uniforms to the "modern school and college girl." The model in the ad is wearing a very typical basketball uniform from the early 1920s—a middie on top and bloomers on the bottom.

This women's team from the early 1920s is ready for a game of basketball in their "athletic" uniforms. In the background of the gym, the windows are boarded up to cover the glare while they play.

(pullover tops with sailor collars), which were paid for by the school. Coaches reminded players to wear underdrawers because the elastic waistband on bloomers was known to weaken. That way a player would be prepared if her bloomers fell off.

Players paid $1.50 for their high cut black leather shoes with elk-skin soles. Spalding charged $1.25 for low-cut shoes. The best shoe, made with a special rubber sole that minimized slipping, sold for $3.50. In the late 1920s and the 1930s, during the Great Depression (a time of a poor economy and unemployment), girls practiced basketball in stocking feet. They saved their shoes for real games.

To tell teams apart, each team wore a different colored sash. Often a player wore a ribbon or hat, such as a tam (a tight-fitting, round, braided cap) or a stocking cap to keep her hair out of her face. Another reason for wearing a hat was to prevent hair pulling. In 1922 the Cresco Lady Saints played in hats with ruffles. A daring player might "bob" her hair, meaning that she cut it short.

By the mid-1940s coaches and players realized that their team's look added to the game and helped sell tickets. Dress, on and off the court, was of great importance. Ruth Lester, wife of an Iowa girls' basketball coach, designed uniforms for her husband's teams. His teams usually qualified to play in state tournaments. Coach Lester's Oakland teams could afford to have new uniforms made. Over the years Mrs. Lester created 10 different sets.

Her first midriff outfit, introduced in 1946, set the style for the next ten years. When spectators saw it, they oohed, aahed, and whistled. Some were shocked because they could see skin between the player's midriff top and shorts. Taller players revealed more skin. The girls yanked at their midriffs to keep them from creeping up too high. Even so, the midriff style caught on.

This New York basketball team from the Savage School in the 1930s is a bit more modern with their "bob" haircuts.

One Lester design featured a halter top, a short top that tied in front and exposed a player's shoulders. Another style looked like the top of a prom dress with shoulder straps. These tops were worn with white satin skirts over panty briefs. Some teams played in satin shorts with elastic hems that hugged their thighs. Satin uniforms might seem extravagant, but satin was a fabric that was readily available during World War II (1939–1945). Other fabrics were

Officials' Uniforms

By 1919 it was determined that the officials' uniforms had to be a different color than those of the players, and they were also required to wear rubber-soled shoes. By the 1930s officials dressed in navy-blue blazers with powder-blue piping and an official's shield on the jacket's breast pocket. In the 1950s female officials wore navy-blue-and-white striped shirts with an updated shield and blue skirts. Culottes, kilts, or slacks were acceptable in the 1970s, but the length of the kilts was regulated. The familiar black-and-white shirts, black slacks, and black shoes and socks of today have been the dress code since 1985.

being used for military purposes. One Iowa team, the Candy Kids of Garnavillo, got their name from their peppermint-striped satin uniforms.

In 1947 the Steamboat Rock High School team in Iowa played in lightweight uniforms made from surplus army parachutes. One spectator reportedly remarked that it was no wonder the team flew across the court so fast.

In the 1950s and 1960s, Iowa teams wore long-sleeved satin jackets with long pants for warm-ups. Players often wore color-coordinated high-top shoes and socks. The girls liked to fold down the top of the sock just over the top of the shoe. New socks held their shape, but once they were washed, the tops stretched and had to be held up with a rubber band. Color-coordinated kneepads completed the "look."

Coaches thought about style, too. One superstitious coach wore his green tie to every game. Another coach dressed in his lucky brown suit for every game, and his team ended up winning the championship. Some coaches appeared at games wearing strange color combinations. Even fans dressed for success, wearing their school colors.

College and Business School Teams

After high school, Iowa girls wanted to continue playing basketball. In 1928 William Penn College organized the first women's college team in Iowa. Some girls chose to go to business or beauty schools that sponsored teams. Others went to work for industries or banks that sponsored teams. Many girls entered the liberal arts college Iowa Wesleyan in Mt. Pleasant because they recruited women for their team, called the Tigerettes. The *Iowa Girls' Basketball Yearbook* printed recruiting ads from businesses and schools that had women's basketball teams. These ads tried to entice women by offering them top competition, travel, and victories in addition to education and career opportunities.

From the 1930s through the 1950s three teams achieved championship status: the American Institute of Business (AIB), the American Institute of Commerce for Stenographers (AIC Stenos), and the Iowa Wesleyan College Tigerettes. AIB formed their team in 1930. In 1934 they held a 22–0 record, beating top high school teams. They played with a white ball, which seemed to be more visible. By the end of the game the ball was often smeared with lipstick.

AIB introduced the rule that allowed a guard to place her hands around the ball while an opponent was shooting a basket. This play was called "tying up the ball." AIB also pioneered the two-dribble rule, which meant a player could bounce the ball two

Half-court Game

In 1936, Iowa girls' and women's teams began playing two-court basketball, also known as half-court. The rest of the country continued playing the three-court game. Half-court players could move around on half the court instead of playing only in assigned sections. When players approached the centerline, they had to stop quickly to avoid stepping over it. They were not allowed to cross into the other half of the court. Six women played on each side: three forwards from one team and three guards from the other team. Only the forwards could shoot baskets. Instead of a center jump after scoring, the ball was given to the opposing team at center court. These changes sped up the game.

times before passing. They were the first Iowa team to play in the National AAU tournament and the first Iowa team to play outside the United States. AIB played in Canada against the "world champion" Edmonton Commercial Grads in 1935, 1937, and 1939.

Student secretaries at AIC in Davenport, Iowa, formed a team called the AIC Stenos in 1937. They won the AAU national championship in 1942 and 1943. In those two years, six Stenos were chosen as AAU All-Americans. Frances Stansberry, a 5-foot 9-inch player, could play either forward or guard. Iowa considered her its first jump shooter. She could shoot with either hand. Fans called her Stansberry the Unstoppable when she played forward and Stansberry the Stopper when she played guard.

In 1942, during World War II, the Stenos played an exhibition game in Toronto, Canada, before 15,000 spectators. They raised $40,000 for the Red Cross, which used it to help British children who were left homeless by the war. The next year the Stenos toured Mexico for 21 days as guests of the government and played several Mexican teams. The tour raised money to buy sewing machines for needy Mexicans. Then in 1949 the Stenos traveled 7,000 miles on a goodwill tour through South and Central America to teach girls how to play basketball. The United States *Congressional Record*, which keeps records of important events, credited the Stenos for contributing to improved relationships with several Latin American countries.

Iowa Wesleyan College had formed a 12-member team called the Tigerettes in 1943. Olan Ruble coached this team as well as men's basketball and football. Two years later the Tigerettes competed in AAU national tournaments. Wesleyan College helped open channels of communication between IGHSAU and AAU. The college held basketball clinics for coaches, players, and officials. Between 1952 and 1962, 25 Tigerettes were named AAU All-Americans, and many were chosen for national teams. To become an All-American, a student had to be a good player and earn good grades. During those ten years, the teams also played in international games.

In 1962 the Tigerettes hosted the women's national team from the USSR. Local and national newspapers covered the game. The college fed the Soviets traditional Iowa food and gave them a tour of the campus. The event was a success, and Wesleyan decided to invite the Peruvian national team the following year.

Coach Ruble was also a member of the Olympic team committee from 1956 to 1976. During those 20 years, he campaigned for women's basketball to be included in the Olympics. In 1976, the same year Ruble retired from the committee, women's basketball became an Olympic event.

Three Outstanding Iowa Players

In the late 1960s, Denise Long, a 5-foot 11-inch forward at Union-Whitten High School, attracted a lot of attention in Iowa. She averaged 51.4 points per game. Another forward, 5-foot 10-inch Jeanette Olson from Everly High School, averaged 51.2 points per game. In 1968 their teams played each other for the state championship. It was the first color telecast of a girls' high school basketball championship game. One newspaper printed this headline: "MISS OLSON, MEET MISS LONG."

A hush filled the gym when they were introduced. Long and Olson hugged each other. Then the battle began. Olson outscored Long. She sank 24 out of

Denise Long, the greatest female basketball player of the time, demonstrates the jump shot she used when she broke an all-time girls' record by scoring 111 points in one game while playing for Union-Whitten High School in Iowa.

25 free throws. Her game total was 76 points. Long scored 64 points. Her cousin Cindy made 41 points. At the end of the game the score was tied 101–101. Overtime brought victory to Union-Whitten, with a score of 113–107. *Sports Illustrated* printed a five-page full-color feature about the game.

Reporters from *Sports Illustrated*, *Chicago Tribune*, *The Wall Street Journal*, *The New York Times*, and *The Boston Globe* interviewed Long. She set all kinds of records. In one game, Long scored 111 points, breaking Irene Silka's record by one point. In one season, she scored 1,986 points. She ended her basketball career with a total of 6,250 points!

In 1969 the San Francisco Warriors, a men's team, selected Long as their thirteenth draft choice. They were the first National Basketball Association (NBA) team to draft a woman. The NBA commissioner did not allow Long to play, but she did get a chance to work out at the Warriors' training camp. The news of the draft prompted more interviews. Johnny Carson, host of *The Tonight Show*, interviewed Long, too. This fulfilled her secret wish to go on television and speak about Iowa girls' basketball.

In 1985 the IGHSAU offered high schools the option of continuing with the six-player divided-court game or changing to the full-court five-player game. Into the 1990s three quarters of the high schools chose to continue playing the six-player game while one quarter picked the five-player option. Iowa held championships for both types of play. (Finally in 1993, Iowa gave up the six-player game.)

Senior Lynne Lorenzen led Ventura High School to a win at the 1987 state championships. She was named Miss Iowa Basketball. During her four years, Lorenzen averaged 60 points per game. Her total career points added up to 6,736, breaking Long's record by 486! After high school, Lorenzen attended Iowa State University on a basketball scholarship and had to learn to play full-court ball.

Since 1900 more than a million girls have played interscholastic basketball in Iowa. When Dr. E. Wayne Cooley became executive secretary of IGHSAU in 1954, he expanded the program from just basketball to include several other sports. His contributions have made IGHSAU the longest-lasting high school athletic association for girls, and it still exists today.

Chapter 4

Travelin' Teams

Around 1910 many companies and industries, like Coca-Cola and textile manufacturers, organized amateur women's and men's basketball teams made up of employees. The main reason they formed teams was to advertise their products. Some of these businesses recruited women by offering them job training and a good salary. Many of these teams played in the Amateur Athletic Union (AAU) tournaments.

Up until 1916 women's basketball teams had scheduled games with other teams that were close by. For instance, a college team might play against a church team, or an industrial team might play against a high school team. In Texas in 1917 the University Interscholastic League was formed to regulate games. Now college teams played other college teams, and industrial teams competed with other industrial teams.

Babe Didrikson and the Dallas Golden Cyclones

Employers Casualty, an insurance company, sponsored the Dallas Golden Cyclones. Melvin J. McCombs, the company's director of women's athletics, managed the team. McCombs named the team after his job, which was handling cyclone claims. He wanted his team to be the best, especially against its rival, the Sunoco Oilers. The Oilers, formerly called the Schepp's Aces, had never lost a tournament or league game from 1927 to 1929. They swept the AAU Championship in 1929 and 1930.

McCombs heard about a 5-foot 6-inch star player in Houston, Texas. Even though he already had ten All-Americans, McCombs traveled to Houston in February 1930 to see her play. There he scouted Mildred "Babe" Didrikson, who played for the Miss Royal Purples High School team of Beaumont, Texas. During that game, Babe impressed McCombs by scoring 26 points.

After the game, McCombs persuaded Didrikson's father to let Babe join the Cyclones. Shortly after, Babe left high school. McCombs met Babe and her father at the Dallas train station in his yellow Cadillac. That night, with no practice, Babe played her first game as a Cyclone. She chose a blue-and-white shirt with number 7 to wear with the belted orange-plaid short shorts. Babe scored 14 of the team's 48 winning points.

The rivalry between the Cyclones and Oilers continued for years. During their regular season of more than 40 games, the Cyclones averaged 38 points per game and kept their opponents to an average of 11 points per game. In the 1930 AAU national

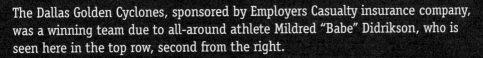

The Dallas Golden Cyclones, sponsored by Employers Casualty insurance company, was a winning team due to all-around athlete Mildred "Babe" Didrikson, who is seen here in the top row, second from the right.

tournament in Wichita, Kansas, Babe averaged 42 points per game. In the semifinals the Oilers beat the Cyclones by one point.

Then Babe started to slack off. She wanted more money because she was the star. Sometimes Coach Danny Lynch benched her, feeling she was not acting like a team player. Still the Cyclones won the 1931 championship by one point. But Babe's average dropped more than 50 percent that season, to 20 points per game.

Here, Babe is showing off her golf skills at a tournament in 1931. After her basketball career she made a living as a professional golfer.

Employers Casualty paid Babe about $900 a year, which was much more than most workers earned with similar or better jobs. Babe sent nearly two-thirds of her salary to her family. By the time she left the team in late 1932, Babe was earning $3,600 a year. That year the Durant Cardinals won the AAU finals.

Babe was an all-around great athlete who participated in many other sports. In the 1932 Olympics, Babe broke world records in the javelin throw and the 80-meter hurdles. She took home two gold medals and one silver medal. Then Babe toured and played basketball exhibition games for two years in small towns with her coed team. Known as the All-Americans, they played 91 games, winning 70 of them. By the 1940s Babe earned a living as a professional golfer. The Associated Press named her Woman Athlete of the Half Century in 1950.

First Black Women's Basketball Teams

During the 1930s black and white people lived in segregated neighborhoods. They were separated from each other at schools, at restaurants, and in sports. Two all-black women's teams, the Wissahickon and the Philadelphia Tribune Hustle, were started in Philadelphia in the 1930s. For nine years the *Philadelphia Tribune*, an all-black newspaper, sponsored the Hustle, who lost only six of their games. Hustle players conducted demonstration games and basketball clinics throughout Philadelphia.

Ora Washington played center for the Hustle for 18 seasons and was one of their top scorers. The year before Washington joined the Hustle, she was captain of the Germantown Hornets. Washington also played tennis. She won eight women's singles titles at the all-black American Tennis Association (ATA) championships.

The Smart Set, an all-black basketball team from Brooklyn, New York, featured Dore Cole and her sisters. In Illinois, Isadore Channels played basketball on the all-black Chicago Romas team. Channels and her teammates dominated the Black Midwest League. Like Ora Washington, Channels was also a tennis champ and won four ATA titles.

All American Red Heads

In the 1930s hairdressers from beauty salons in the Cassville, Missouri, area put together a basketball team. Jo and Geneva Langerman, twin members of the team, were natural redheads. For fun, the other players mixed up henna dye and massaged it into their hair. After their hair dried, they admired its new red color. The team called themselves the Cassville Red Heads. Later on, they chose ready-to-mix Clairol Flame #33S to dye their hair.

Doyle Olson owned the salons and knew about basketball from her husband, C. M. "Ole" Olson. He had played on an exhibition team called Olson's Terrible Swedes. Soon C. M. Olson managed and promoted the Cassville Red Heads, renamed the Missouri Red Heads by the end of 1935. Under his guidance, the Red Heads improved their skills and learned to perform comical routines. They charged 25 to 40 cents admission for their games. Once while recruiting, Olson told a reporter he was looking for tall, good-looking women who could play basketball.

C. M. Olson also owned a women's farm team, the Ozark Hillbillies. The purpose of a farm team was to give amateur players a chance to improve their skills and gain playing experience. Eventually, some of those players became Red Heads.

At times there were three different Red Head teams barnstorming, or traveling from town to town to play games. Sometimes the Red Heads played army camp teams or amateur men's teams, using men's rules. This meant five players on each team played full court with continuous dribbling.

One of the teams made a trip to the Philippines in the 1940s just before American entry into World War II. When the United States warned Americans to leave the island, the team boarded a cattle boat and left, escorted by the military. Eventually, they arrived safely back in America.

In the late 1940s, Olson asked high school coach Orwell Moore and his wife, Lorene Moore, a basketball player, to manage the team that traveled throughout the West. Many All-American stars from the AAU had joined the Red Heads. One of the original Red Heads, Peggy Lawson Surface, told Doyle Olson that since there were so many All-Americans on the team, they should be called the All American Red Heads. In 1950, C. M. Olson agreed and copyrighted the name.

The Red Heads grew from a small town beauty salon team into a highly skilled and privately owned organization. Some historians credit the Red Heads as being the first professional women's basketball team. Often they played every night for six months out of the year. By 1950 the Red Heads had played 169 men's teams, winning 129 of the games.

The 1955 All American Red Heads wear their flashy uniforms during a prematch warm-up game. The Red Heads were highly entertaining as well as skillful and clever ball players.

In 1947 the Red Heads piled into their station wagon, "Nellie J. Bly," which they had named after the famous journalist and adventurer of the 1880s. They traveled through 38 states playing 180 games. Sometimes the players referred to the wagon as "She Has To," meaning, she has to have gas, she has to have tires, she has to have water and oil. Other times the Red Heads barnstormed across the country in style, riding in a 31-foot stretch Oldsmobile.

Most years the Red Heads wore red, white, and blue uniforms with red lipstick, blue eye shadow, and perfume. In the mid-1950s they wore short satin skirts, midriff tops, and red sneakers with kneepads and knee-high socks. Off the court the Red Heads always dressed conservatively.

Before a game, they blew kisses at the fans. Sometimes they introduced themselves to their opponents, stroked their hands, and flattered them. It was all part of the entertainment. When the whistle blew, the Red Heads became serious and called out play patterns.

Turn On the Lights

During their 50 years of touring, the All American Red Heads had more than 100 players and won 100 or more games a year. They came a long way from playing on dance floors and skating rinks and in factories. In some places the lighting was so poor at the game that lanterns were held up in the rafters so the players could see. During one game the electricity went out due to an ice storm. Fans had a choice to either turn on their car headlights to shine through the open doors and windows or go home. The fans chose to light up the building and the Red Heads played. They played because they loved the game.

During the first part of a game, they played strongly. Then as the game progressed, the Red Heads would distract the men's teams by performing trick plays, routines, and telling jokes. Some Red Heads could dribble with their knees, shoot on their knees, or spin the ball on their fingers. One player could dribble two balls blindfolded. Allegra "Stubby" Winters, a 5-foot 4-inch player in the 1940s, confused her opponents by dribbling between 6-foot 4-inch Gene Love's legs. Sometimes Stubby would shoot while riding piggyback on another player.

When Lorene Moore played, she wowed audiences at halftime by spinning a basketball on one finger of each hand at the same time. She could bounce the ball off her head and into the basket. Moore scored more than 35,000 points during her 11-year career.

The Red Heads performed other antics, including tricky dribbling and passing routines. Zethel Keith, a 1950s player, would stop at the foul line, fake passes, set the ball down, and go for a fake hook shot, which her opponents would try to block. While the other team stood around confused, she would pick up the ball and go in for an easy layup. Another favorite routine was called "La Conga Out-of-Bounds." (The conga is a dance that started in Latin America.) The Red Heads would form a long winding conga line and dance across the court with the ball.

Willa Faye "Red" Mason, a 1950s player, pleased the crowds when she placed the ball between her ankles, jumped up, and kicked her legs back. The ball flew over her head and usually sank into the basket. Sometimes Red would stop dribbling during a game, go into the crowd, and shake hands with a male admirer.

Donna "Spanky" Losier played for the Red Heads in the 1970s. She was a fine outside shooter, excellent dribbler, and passed the ball unselfishly. Losier also entertained the crowd with the "Big Pinch"—starting a commotion by bumping into a male player and then telling the referee he pinched her. To get laughs, Losier opened her "Crazy Kit," took out a sequin-covered whistle and top hat, and ran around the court with a giant powder puff. Her team liked to mimic the referee just to get attention from the fans.

One 1970s team of Red Heads called their car "Big Whitey." To avoid cliques, Coach Moore required the women to sit next to a different player during each trip. He also didn't allow the same two women to continually room together.

Moore claimed it cost $140,000 a year for the team to tour. The players split $40,000 as their income. Along with health insurance, it was a fairly good income for seven months. Moore bragged, "Every day is Christmas when you're an All American Red Head."

Operating expenses were minimal. Moore didn't have to rent a gym because the Red Heads were always the visiting team. Therefore, there was no cost for electricity, insurance, or referees, which were part of the home team's expenses. Advertising was free because when the Red Heads came to town, it was big news.

Moore made sure his players knew the schedule about a month ahead of time, and they were sworn to secrecy. If news leaked out any sooner, Moore worried that another event would be scheduled at the same time, which meant less income for the Red Heads. Coach Moore recalled that his team once played for 11,500 fans at the Chicago Stadium.

Playing in a different town every night could get lonely. In December 1973 the team spent Christmas in a motel in Joplin, Missouri. They managed to find a small tree, which they decorated with shaving cream. For entertainment they held a Miss America contest and awarded the winner a pickle. The women toasted the day with Coca-Cola and Dr Pepper.

Several famous Red Heads appeared on television shows like *The Ed Sullivan Show* and *I've Got a Secret*. They were guests on late-night talk shows hosted by Jay Leno and David Letterman, as well as Rosie O'Donnell's daytime show. The last team stopped playing in 1986 with a 114–21 record. From 1930 to 1980 the Red Heads raised thousands of dollars for charities and schools.

Hazel Walker and the Arkansas Travelers

Before becoming a Red Head in 1945, Hazel Walker, of Cherokee descent, received a full scholarship to play basketball for Tulsa Business College in Oklahoma. During her amateur career, she was named an AAU All-American seven times. The Associated Press selected her as the 1940 Female Athlete of the Year. During halftime at a game in 1944, Walker amazed fans by making 50 free throws in a row. Over the years, she won six National Free Throw Championships.

In 1949, Walker formed her own team, the Arkansas Travelers. When conducting tryouts, she looked for skilled players who were poised and attractive. Walker made sure her players acted and dressed nicely in public. The Travelers challenged men's teams, but they played a more serious game than the Red Heads. They won 85 percent of their games. During halftime, Walker held free throw contests.

The Travelers barnstormed from 1949 to 1965. They played six games a week and earned about $200 a month. The team's management paid for the hotel rooms, but the women had to buy their own food and uniforms. They drove to the games in a station wagon paid for by Walker's Red Head earnings. The players threw their luggage onto the rack on top of the car and crammed themselves inside. In those days some people thought that women traveling without a male escort was inappropriate and probably unsafe. To protect themselves from possible robberies, the team carried a gun.

Privately owned teams, like the Red Heads, and AAU teams, like the Cyclones, were the pioneer teams of the 1930s that brought much needed attention to women's basketball. However, the 1940s and 1950s produced three powerhouse AAU teams: Hanes Hosiery, Nashville Business College, and the Flying Queens. Players on these women's basketball teams raised the game to a higher level.

Seeing Double-Double

The basketball term "double-double" has double meanings. A player could have double digits in scoring, rebounds, or assists. If a player made 12 points and 10 assists or 12 points and 10 rebounds those would be double-doubles. Twin basketball players are another kind of double. Many times they perceive what the other one is about to do on the court and act on it by coordinating a play. Twins elevate the meaning of teamwork.

Redheaded twins Geneva and Josephine Langerman were known as the "first ladies of Iowa girls' basketball." They played high school ball in the early 1930s. Coaches and players of other teams knew they would probably lose when they played against these twins. Both girls could handle the ball, shoot well, and closely guard their opponents.

In the 1970s, Lynette and Lynnea Sjoquist, another pair of redheaded twins, wrote to Orwell Moore, asking to play with the Red Heads. The 6-foot 1-inch 20-year-olds from Minnesota joined the team in 1973. They had to learn to handle the fast passes of the seasoned players.

Twins Faye and Kaye Young played for North Carolina State University in the late 1970s on full scholarships. After college the twins played for the Women's Basketball League's New York Stars. Dannon Yogurt hired the 5-foot 10-inch twins to do television commercials.

Pamela and Paula McGee played for the University of Southern California, winning the National Collegiate Athletic Association championships in 1983 and 1984. Pam, a two-time Kodak All-American, earned a gold medal at the 1984 Olympics, which she gave to her sister. A consistent scorer and defender, Pam was the second draft pick for the first season of the Women's National Basketball Association's (WNBA's) Sacramento Monarchs. Paula played for the Women's American Basketball Association's Dallas Diamonds.

Blond twins Heidi and Heather Burge from California received full scholarships to the University of Virginia and played in three Final Four championship games. According to the *Guinness Book of World Records*, the Burges are the tallest female identical twins, at 6 feet 5 inches. Heather joined the Monarchs in 1999, and Heidi joined the WNBA's Los Angeles Sparks for one season. Later Heidi was traded to the WNBA's Washington Mystics and then retired because of a back injury. In 2002 Disney created a TV movie, *Double Teamed*, based on their lives.

Coco and Kelly Miller, 5-foot 10-inch twin players at the University of Georgia, caught and passed the ball at such speed that opponents had to play hard defense. Always full of energy, the twins scrambled for loose balls and made steals. They became the first pair of athletes to receive the James E. Sullivan Memorial Award, given to athletes who show outstanding personal and athletic achievement.

In 2001, Kelly joined the WNBA's Charlotte Sting, and Coco joined the Mystics. As with all twins, there are differences between the two. Kelly likes to shoot from the field. Coco prefers to take it to the basket, and she reties her shoes two or three times before a game because she is superstitious.

When the Miller twins graduated from the University of Georgia, the Brown-Braxton twins replaced them. In high school, Kara, a 6-foot 6-inch center, became the first sophomore to be chosen Oregon's Player of the Year. Kim, a 6-foot 2-inch forward, excelled as a defender and rebounder.

The Dosty twins played for the Gaels at St. Mary's College in California. Jermisha, a 6-foot 3-inch center, had double-doubles in 15 games in 2000. In her senior year "Misha" earned the 2002 West Coast Conference (WCC) Defender of the Year honors and was picked to play for the Sacramento Monarchs. Jerkisha, a 6-foot 2-inch Gaels forward, made ten double-doubles in 2000. "Kisha" was named the 2002 WCC Player of the Year.

Chapter 5

On the Road and in the Air

In 1956 hundreds of women went to St. Joseph, Missouri, to compete in the annual AAU Women's National Basketball Championship. The women were members of teams with great names like the Dairy Maids, Pine-Sol Queens, and Real Refrigeration.

They attended the Sunday breakfast given by the Junior Chamber of Commerce. Games continued throughout the day. On Monday night, as the band played at the opening ceremonies, the well-groomed teams marched into the gym. On Tuesday evening the AAU tournament beauty queen was crowned.

A radio station broadcast the five-day hardwood classic with play-by-play calls. Radio and TV announcers interviewed coaches and players. Newspapers covered the game, too. During the week, players entered the free throw contest. At the end of the championship game, the Most Valuable Player (MVP) and the All-Americans were selected. The Flying Queens took home the Championship Trophy.

Hanes Hosiery Girls

In the 1940s in Winston-Salem, North Carolina, the Hanes Hosiery Mill, an industry that manufactured women's stockings, sponsored basketball teams for its employees. Hanes built a gym that held 2,000 spectators. The men's and women's teams practiced after work anywhere from 4 to 9 P.M. Sometimes they played outside on nearby dirt courts during lunch. For 25 cents fans packed the gym to watch the Hanes teams play.

Hanes hired a coach, a manager, and a nurse for the women's team, the Hanes Hosiery Girls. The mill expected the women to work their shift and play games. Some of the women players worked in the office. Others worked as seamstresses. Hanes arranged the women's schedules so all the players would be off work at the same time.

Virgil Yow proved to be a tough coach for the Hanes Girls. Before coaching them, he had coached a men's team at High Point College in North Carolina. Yow worked his female players as hard as he did his male players. To improve their accuracy with free throws, Yow made the women shoot at a basket that was gradually raised. The Hanes team often played against local high school boys' teams for practice.

Yow recruited 6-foot 2-inch teenager Eunies Futch from Florida in 1947. When she was in 11th grade, Futch had played for an independent team in Florida. She graduated from high school on January 15, 1947, and within five days she was working at Hanes and playing her first game for them. Futch became their star forward and was named an AAU All-American three times.

Basketball player Evelyn "Eckie" Jordan, who was a foot shorter than Futch, led her high school team to victory at the South Carolina state championships in 1942. After high school, she worked for the local mill and played basketball on its team. In 1948, Jordan heard that Hanes was recruiting, so she headed 500 miles north. Jordan convinced Yow that she was a quick ball handler, great guard, and could make off-balance shots. While a Hanes player, Jordan became a five-time AAU All-American.

From 1948 to 1950 the Hanes Girls lost in the quarter finals of the AAU championship to Nashville Business College (NBC) of Tennessee. In 1951 they beat the Flying Queens of Wayland College of Texas to win the championship. Futch dominated the game with great defense and rebounds. Hanes won over Iowa's AIC in 1952.

Hanes grabbed its third AAU championship against the Flying Queens in 1953, but lost to them in 1954. Up until then the team had won 102 games in a row. Hanes gave three pairs of hosiery to each player after winning their championships. Even with all this success, an article in the *Industrial Sports Journal* labeled women's teams "fem squads" and reported that the Hanes Girls would never be as good as men in sports.

The Hanes Hosiery championship team from 1951 includes some well-known members: Coach Yow is in the back row, middle, Eunies Futch stands to his right, and Evelyn "Eckie" Jordan is crouching in the front row, first from the left.

The Hanes Girls and other teams had to constantly adjust to rule changes. Starting in 1949 dribbling twice was legal. A guard was allowed to use her arms, legs, or body to block an opponent, but no physical contact was permitted. By 1951 coaches were allowed to talk to their players during time-outs.

Even though the Hanes Girls had disbanded by 1955, Jordan and Futch continued playing ball. They led the U.S. team to victory at the first Pan American games for women. When they retired from basketball, they shared an apartment and continued working for Hanes Hosiery.

In the mid-1950s, Coach Yow retired, too. He found it difficult to recruit women for his team. His players left to get married, or they quit because their husbands didn't want them to play basketball. As other textile teams disbanded, competitions were becoming scarce.

First International Competitions

In 1953 the United States formed a national team made up of AAU champions to play in the first Fédérale Internationale de Basketball Association (FIBA) World Championships in Chile. The United States beat Chile, winning the title and a huge trophy. (The trophy had to be left behind because it was too big to fit in the plane!) In 1955 women's basketball also became part of the international Pan American Games (created in 1951). Both of these international competitions are still held every four years.

Tennessee AAU Champs of the Mid-1940s

During the Hanes era (1944–1949), a rival team, the Nashville Vultee Aircraft, won five AAU championships. The team was renamed the Vultee Convac Bomberettes and then the Cook's Goldblumes. Margaret Sexton Gleaves, a Goldblumes player, became an eight-time All-American. At the 1948 AAU tournament she was named MVP for her outstanding defense and presented with a gold watch.

Alline Banks Sprouse also played on these championship teams. She could shoot from anywhere on the court and became the team's top scorer. One time, in an All-Star game, she played with her right arm taped to her side because of an injury from the night before. During that game, the right-handed Banks Sprouse shot with her left hand and scored 56 points! Banks Sprouse was named All-American eleven times and voted AAU Most Valuable Player (MVP) nine times.

The Flying Queens

In 1947 ten female students at Wayland Baptist College in Plainview, Texas, formed a basketball team. The obvious choice for a coach was Harley Redin, Wayland's athletic director and men's basketball coach. The newly formed Wayland Queens played against nearby high schools, winning seven games and losing five.

The selection of Queens players was based on the three "Bs": brains, beauty, and ball handling. Coach Redin considered ball handling more important than beauty. However, the Wayland faculty emphasized brains, or academics, over athletics. Like other college girls, the players won scholastic, literary, and beauty honors as well as offices in student organizations.

In 1948, Wayland Baptist College offered travel and scholarships to women in AAU basketball. This was unheard of in those days. The college held tryouts during two weeks in the summer. A woman who made the team got a scholarship and a brand new convertible. The players signed contracts promising not to smoke, drink, or dance, which were the rules set by Wayland Baptist College.

That year Sam Allen took over coaching duties. The team changed its name to the Harvest Queens in 1949 because the Harvest Queen Mill donated money for their uniforms. It was the first year the team played in the National AAU Women's Tournament. After losing their second game, they were out of the tournament.

In 1950 the school's president, Dr. J. W. Marshall, found a new sponsor in Claude Hutcherson, a Wayland alumnus and wealthy oilman. Hutcherson owned an air service with a fleet of Beechcraft Bonanza airplanes. Four of his planes transported the team to games in the United States and to their first international game in Mexico. Mr. Hutcherson and Coach Redin each flew planes. Mrs. Hutcherson, who was also a pilot, chaperoned the team. The 12-member team was now called the Hutcherson Flying Queens.

The Hutchersons pampered the team. They hired award-winning New York hair stylists. The Hutchersons bought the team warm-up outfits and three sets of uniforms in their school colors—blue, gold, and white. At the end of the season they gave each player a sweater with the school letter W sewn on it.

However, the players usually bought their own traveling outfits. For example, one year each woman wore a beige blouse decorated with her monogram and a chocolate-colored skirt for special social occasions. For casual wear they dressed in white blouses and dark blue skirts with bobby socks and loafers. Wherever the Queens went, they presented themselves with poise and style.

In the early 1950s the Queens, who had several All-American players, failed to win an AAU championship. In 1954, during the last minute of the final game of the National AAU Championship against the Kansas City Dons, Faye Wilson sunk two free throws. When the buzzer sounded, the scoreboard read Queens 39, Dons 38. Their luck had changed. The Flying Queens started a 131-game winning streak.

After winning their second national title in 1955, the Queens were honored with a parade and a school holiday. When the Queens won their third AAU title in 1956 against NBC, Wayland Baptist College honored them, but the team received little attention in newspapers. In those days, newspaper coverage for women's basketball was minimal.

In 1956, Harley Redin once again coached the Queens. He made his players run a lot of laps for conditioning. During pregame warm-ups, he had the Queens practice tricky ball handling. Redin emphasized self-control, rules, and aggressive play. After the Queens won their fourth AAU championship in 1957 against Iowa Wesleyan College,

Black Women's Teams in the AAU

Until 1955 no all-black women's teams had competed in AAU tournaments. That year the Z Ramblers placed second in the Northeastern AAU tournament. The Philander-Smith College team from Arkansas fared even better. They had "Big Mo" Arledge from Missouri, who averaged 21 points a game. Philander-Smith won the state AAU championship and went on to the nationals. Arledge was the first black woman player to be chosen for the AAU All-American team.

Wayland fans and the Hutchersons rewarded Coach Redin with a station wagon and a food freezer.

Redin played a large role in changing the rules of women's basketball. He influenced the AAU to allow unlimited dribbling, to change to a five-player full-court game, and to institute the 30-second clock, which limited the amount of time players had to shoot the ball.

In 1957, Patsy Neal, who lived in Georgia, read that the Flying Queens won the AAU championship. She wrote to the college and asked if she could try out for the team. In her letter she mentioned that she had averaged more than 40 points per game in her senior year and made All-State. Neal made the team and earned a full basketball scholarship. When she was a freshman at Wayland, she won the National Free Throw Championship, sinking 48 out of 50 shots.

During the early 1960s, with the help of physical education leaders, rule revisions brought women's basketball to an even higher level. Two players or rovers—one per team—were permitted to cross the line to play full court. They were allowed to dribble three times and steal the ball.

National Business College

While attending George Peabody College for Teachers in Nashville in 1955, Nera White was recruited by National Business College (NBC) to play as a rover. Since Peabody didn't have a team, White agreed to play for NBC. In return, NBC paid for her room and board during her years at Peabody. White was considered an all-around player. She thought teamwork was more important than becoming the highest scorer. The 6-foot 1-inch guard had speed. She could dribble, shoot, rebound, assist, and steal. White could tip in the ball up to 10 feet away from the basket. In the 1950s and 1960s people didn't think women were able to do what White did.

White continued to play for NBC after graduation. Herman O. Balls, the NBC organizer, paid White a dollar an hour to work in his print shop. He also paid her for games and practices. During her 1955–1969 career, White was named AAU All-American 15 times and MVP 10 times. In 1957, as a member of the U.S. team, she won a gold medal at the World Championship games in Brazil. Then in 1992 White was honored as one of the first women to be inducted into the Naismith Memorial Basketball Hall of Fame. Some gyms and highways in Tennessee are named after her.

At 5 feet 11 inches, Joan Crawford (not the movie actress) led her high school team to three state championships. In 1957, NBC recruited her to play as a rover. Her teammates admired her sportsmanship and skills at rebounding and passing. She led the team in scoring and rebounds. Crawford was named MVP in 1963 and 1964 and became an All-American 13 times. She won three gold medals playing on the U.S. team at the World Championship and Pan American games.

Together, White and Crawford led NBC to 96 straight wins. Between 1950 and 1969 NBC won 11 AAU titles under the guidance of Coach John Head. In 1956 each NBC team member received engraved AAU medals. Those who were All-Americans took home a gold basketball.

The fabulous Flying Queens and NBC ruled the 1950s and 1960s. Fans drove hundreds of miles to watch these teams play. Redin coached the Queens for 18 years, and Head coached NBC for 23 years. Their teams met on the court 63 times. The Queens won 32 of those games and NBC won 31. But NBC ended the Flying Queens' 131-game winning streak by beating them in a semifinal game of the 1958 National AAU Women's Tournament.

Change Is in the Air

The 1960s brought change for women in society and at work. Women were pushing harder than ever to be treated equally. In 1962, Eleanor Roosevelt, the wife of former

Joan Crawford (middle) played with the National Business College from 1957 to 1969. She won ten championships with NBC and was named All-American for 13 consecutive seasons. Crawford was enshrined in the Women's Basketball Hall of Fame in 1999.

president Franklin D. Roosevelt, chaired a commission on the status of women and helped to create legislation that promoted equal opportunities and pay.

Women in sports had also been given fewer opportunities than men. For example, men were given funds and more practice time in gyms. Fortunately, with support from the Division of Girls and Women in Sports (DGWS) of the American Association for Health, Physical Education, and Recreation, many high schools and colleges started sports competitions for women. Lack of funding for these programs was a problem. The players had to earn their own money to buy uniforms. They washed cars and sold baked goods. Some coaches paid for their transportation, meals, and other needs out of their own pockets.

One major change in the late 1960s occurred when the Queens selected their first black players, Claudia Menefee and Mary Tulia. Another big improvement occurred in 1966. The AAU allowed unlimited dribbling in women's games. Then finally in 1971, teams of five players ran the whole court and used a 30-second shot clock. H. O. Balls disagreed with the five-player game and chose to dissolve his team. The NBC glory days were over.

In 1967 the Association for Intercollegiate Athletics for Women (AIAW) was developed to govern women's sports. They set guidelines and sponsored national championships. By 1972 female coaches ran the organization. The 1970s were a turning point for women's sports.

Chapter 6

The Spectacular 1970s

In the early 1970s the ratio of high school boys compared to girls who played in a sports program was 12:1. Many schools spent 99 percent of their athletic budget on men's sports programs and only 1 percent on women's programs. Several spectacular events during this decade helped improve the statistics for women in sports.

The First Nationals

The first Invitational Women's Intercollegiate Basketball Tournament was held in 1969. Carol Eckman, coach at West Chester State, a small teachers' college in Pennsylvania, organized the tournament. Eckman's goal was to provide an opportunity for women to play and share information about teams, strategies, and schools. The tournament would determine the women's national champion. Eckman charged a $25 entry fee in order to pay the officials and buy awards.

Carol Eckman

Carol Eckman was born in 1938 in Berlin, Pennsylvania. She became an All-American in 1966. At West Chester State she coached a 62–4 record. When she was coaching, she urged her players to watch men's games on TV and to read a book written by the UCLA men's coach, John Wooden, about basketball. Eckman, also known as "Mother of National Collegiate Championships," died of cancer in 1985. The Women's Basketball Coaches Association honored Eckman in 1986 by creating the Carol Eckman Award, presented to a coach who most represents sportsmanship, ethical behavior, and commitment to students, qualities Eckman lived by.

Sixteen teams participated in the first nationals at West Chester. Iowa Wesleyan walked onto the court in purple satin uniforms. The West Chester Ramettes wore one-piece jumpsuits with Peter-Pan-collared blouses. Western Carolina wore pinnies (sleeve-less, side-less tops with ties or elastic strips that fasten the back and the front together at the waist) over white Bermuda-type shorts and T-shirts.

In the final game of the tournament West Chester played against Western Carolina and won. At the second nationals Cal State Fullerton beat West Chester. The 1971 tournament marked a historical milestone for women's basketball. Mississippi College for Women and West Chester played full court with five-player rules. Mississippi won.

Title IX

A big break for women came from a law, signed by President Richard Nixon, known as Title IX of the Federal Education Amendment of 1972. It said that high schools and colleges that received federal assistance would have to give equal funds to educational and athletic programs for men and women. Shortly afterward, Canada and Australia passed similar laws. Title IX also stated that changes in women's programs had to be made by 1978. Progress was slow. Teams formed. Schools purchased new equipment and scheduled games with other schools, giving more girls opportunities to play competitively.

The Mighty Macs

During the early 1970s, the Mighty Macs from Immaculata, a small college in Pennsylvania, made their mark in women's basketball. The Macs played in pleated tunics with round-collared blouses. Their coach, Cathy Rush, ran a two-hour practice of defensive skills and drills. Her technique worked, and the Macs excelled. The team improved even more after Rush recruited Theresa Shank, a 5-foot 11-inch center with speed and responsiveness. Rush had coached Shank at Cardinal O'Hara High School in Springfield, Pennsylvania, the year before.

Cathy Rush

Cathy Rush, born in 1943, earned degrees at West Chester State. During some Mighty Mac games, Rush's husband, an NBA referee, sat high up in the bleachers. He would give his wife advice about the game via a walkie-talkie. Rush started the Future Star USA camps, which have given hundreds of girls a chance to work with college coaches.

First National Women's Award

Before the mid-1970s the concept of star players was frowned upon. Giving awards and recognition to female basketball players was considered exploitation of women. In 1976 the Eastman Kodak Company, a camera and film manufacturer, created the Kodak All-American Award. It was the first national award presented to top female players. Kodak sponsored women's basketball championships and the first Women's Basketball Coaches Clinic. Coaches from different geographic regions nominated players for the All-American Award. After viewing the nominee's videotapes, another committee of coaches chose the All-Americans.

In 1972 the Macs made it to the AIAW championship playoffs. The team accepted donations for travel expenses to Illinois, where they beat West Chester. The following year the Macs struggled in the semifinals against Southern Connecticut State University. With eight minutes left the Macs trailed by eight points. Shank grabbed 25 rebounds and the Macs kept scoring. In the final seconds Mac guard Marianne Crawford just missed a shot. Shank jumped up and tipped it in. The Macs went on to win the nationals over Queens College of New York, 59–52.

The Macs beat Mississippi College at the 1974 AIAW championships and attracted major newspaper and magazine coverage. In January 1975, a regular season game in which the Macs beat the University of Maryland was televised. A month later the Macs beat Queens College in front of 12,000 fans at Madison Square Garden in New York City. This marked the first time that women's intercollegiate basketball was played there. The team's success may have encouraged other colleges to award scholarship money for women.

Margaret Wade Rescues Delta State

Margaret Wade played basketball for Delta State. During her senior year, in 1932, the university decided to drop the women's basketball program. The school administrators thought the game was "too strenuous for young ladies." Wade remembered when she and her teammates cried and burned their uniforms.

In 1959, Wade returned to Delta as the physical education director. When the university reinstated the basketball program in 1973, they asked Wade, who was nearly 60 years old, to coach the women's team. The players and their families embraced her caring attitude, discipline, and sense of humor. By the time Wade retired in 1979, she had racked up a 157–23 college record. She coached Delta State to three AIAW titles.

The Wade Trophy was established for Margaret Wade, who began coaching women's basketball at Delta State University when she was 60 years old.

Because of Wade's contributions to women's basketball, the Wade Trophy was established. The award is given to a female Kodak All-American player for academics, player performance, and community service. The first trophy was presented to Carol Blazejowski from Montclair State College in New Jersey in 1978.

Blazejowski, a 5-foot 10-inch forward, could always find the open spot, and once she got the ball, she became a scoring machine. From 1974 to 1978, "Blaze" racked up 3,199 points. In her senior year she averaged 38.6 points per game. Blaze also held the record for a career average of 31.7 points per game. She was named Kodak All-American three times. During a game at Madison Square Garden against Queens College, Blaze set another record by scoring 52 points.

Lusia Harris and Delta State

In 1974, Lusia Harris was about to enroll at Alcorn A&M (Agricultural and Mechanical), a black college in Mississippi with no basketball team. Then along came Coach Margaret Wade. She recruited 6-foot 3-inch Harris, an all-around player with an exceptional inside jump, for Delta State University. Although Delta State had no athletic scholarships, they managed to offer Harris academic and federal scholarships. Harris accepted and played center for Delta State's Lady Statesmen from 1974 to 1977.

At the 1975 AIAW tournament, Delta State played in the finals. That

Lusia Harris was a three-time All-American at Delta State, which had an incredible record of 109–5 during her four years there. She was the first player to win the Broderick Cup for Outstanding Women's Basketball Player in the United States, and the first player to score a basket in women's Olympic history.

year marked the first time that an all-black team, the Federal City College team from Washington, D.C., competed. During the game against Immaculata, Delta State guard Debbie Brock became stressed and vomited on the sidelines. Lusia Harris stepped up to the challenge and played an outstanding game. The Lady Statesmen halted the previous AIAW tournament winners, the Mighty Macs, 90–81. The game was televised at a later time.

In her junior year, Harris averaged 30 points per game, with a career average of 25.9. She led her team to two more national championships and was chosen the tournament MVP for three seasons in a row. In 1976, Harris set a record of 47 points at a game played at Madison Square Garden against Queens College.

Fans couldn't get enough of Harris and the Lady Statesmen. When they traveled to away games, the fans wore T-shirts that said "Lady Statesmen are Dyn-O-Mite." Often when the players returned home to Cleveland, Mississippi, a police escort led them through town. Along the way 50 to 60 carloads of fans formed a car parade. Delta State became known as the "little school that was good."

Pump Up the Volume

To cheer on their team, the Mighty Macs fans beat wooden sticks on metal buckets, and the Lady Statesmen fans banged wooden blocks. Players had to work at staying focused because of the noisy fans. Since then, artificial noisemakers have been banned at all games.

Honda Broderick Award

In 1977 two awards were created by Thomas Broderick, a sports apparel business owner. The Broderick Award was given to the AIAW player of the year in each sport. The Broderick Cup was awarded to the best overall AIAW athlete from all sports. Lusia Harris became the first woman basketball player to receive both awards. In 1987 Honda Motor Company began to sponsor the awards.

Ann Meyers Makes News

Athletic scholarships for women were rare. Title IX stated that if a college offered athletic scholarships to men, it also had to offer them to women. Some small colleges in the South that didn't have football teams (most athletic scholarship money went to football players in the Southern states) used their budgets to recruit and offer athletic scholarships to female basketball players in the early 1970s. These offers attracted top players, and soon small-school teams like Delta State University were winning the AIAW national championships.

But in 1974 the University of California at Los Angeles (UCLA) offered Ann Meyers a full four-year athletic scholarship. When a major university like UCLA gives a full athletic scholarship to a woman, it sends a message all over the world that it's time to provide equal opportunities to women in sports.

Meyers was already well known in southern California. In elementary school she had played basketball on a boys' team. Her parents had gone to the school board to fight for her right to play. Meyers had developed into a high jumper, long-range shooter, and brilliant passer. She was named the first four-time Kodak All-American in 1978, as well as the Broderick Award and Broderick Cup winner. UCLA retired her number 15 jersey.

After college, Meyers became the first female NBA draftee with the Indiana Pacers. Although she was cut from the team, she was guaranteed a salary of $50,000 to become a Pacers broadcaster. Later on, Meyers chose to play in the Women's Basketball League (WBL). She played two seasons and twice earned MVP trophies. The second season she signed for $50,000. In the late 1970s Meyers organized an AAU team of her own, Annie's Bananas. They won the national championships from 1977 to 1979.

Women's Wheelchair Basketball

After World War II, wounded American soldiers started playing wheelchair basketball in California. The first U.S. women's wheelchair basketball team formed in 1970. They were called the Illinois Ms. Kids and played for the University of Illinois at Champaign-Urbana. Five years later, the National Women's Wheelchair Basketball Tournament (NWWBT) started. The Fighting Illini (formerly Illinois Ms. Kids) won many of the tournaments.

Another wheelchair team called the Los Angeles Sparks won three NWWBT championships (1999–2001). A thrill for these winners was having their team photo on boxes of Team Cheerios cereal.

Wheelchair teams also played internationally. The U.S. women's team won the gold for basketball in the 1988 Paralympics. Like the Olympics, the Paralympics occur every four years. The 1st Roosevelt World Wheelchair Basketball Challenge (now called the Roosevelt Cup) began in 2000.

During the final 2000 Roosevelt game, the United States trailed Canada by 11 points with less than six minutes left to play. Miriam Nibley tossed the ball to Josie Johnson, who wheeled down the court to make the shot and was fouled. When the buzzer sounded at the end of the game, the teams were tied. In overtime the United States continued to score and beat top-ranked Canada, 47–38.

Wheelchair Rules

Many players on wheelchair teams are paraplegics, who cannot move the lower part of their bodies. The players are classified according to their injury or disability. Each team is made up of players with various degrees of disabilities.

There are height, seat cushion, and various wheelchair equipment regulations. The rules for disabled players are somewhat different than in regular basketball. For example:

• Players with the ball are allowed four seconds in the lane.

• Traveling is called if a player pushes her wheelchair three times without dribbling.

• A foul is called if a player elevates herself out of the seat. The other team then gets two free throws and takes the ball out-of-bounds.

Feel the Vibe

In Washington, D.C., the Bisons, a women's team at Gallaudet University, don't shout out their plays. These players communicate with sign language because they are deaf. Their visual focus controls their plays. Bison fans cheer them on by stamping their feet, and the players feel the vibrations.

In 2001, Ronda Jo Miller, a graduate of Gallaudet, became the first deaf female pro basketball player for a team in Denmark. Miller, a 6-foot 2-inch forward, joined the WNBA's Washington Mystics in 2002.

Nancy Lieberman Makes News

The 1970s produced another female basketball star, 5-foot 10-inch Nancy Lieberman. In 1976 at age seventeen, this high school basketball phenomenon made the Olympic team and became the youngest basketball player to win an Olympic medal. Before that Lieberman had played street ball in Harlem, New York, against top male players. On the streets Lieberman improved her quickness, no-look passing, shooting skills, and rebounding.

At Old Dominion University (ODU) in Norfolk, Virginia, she led her team to two AIAW national championships. Lieberman became a natural point guard. She earned the nickname "Lady Magic" for her fancy ball-handling skills. Her career points totaled 2,430. Lieberman was named All-American three times. She became the

Old Dominion's Nancy Lieberman in action against Union College in November 1979.

only two-time winner of the Wade Trophy and was twice named a Broderick Cup winner. In the 1980s she played with a WBL team in Dallas and later joined the Women's American Basketball Association (WABA) league.

At age 28 Lieberman became the first woman to play in a men's pro league. She played in the United States Basketball League (USBL), a summer league for NBA hopefuls, for three summers, each on different teams. However, Lieberman played less than 12 minutes a game and averaged just one point and one assist. She learned how tough it was to play on a men's team. She had the desire and knowledge of the game but lacked the speed, strength, and size to compete against men.

Lieberman as coach of WNBA's Detroit Shock in 1999. She's now considered one of the most skilled players ever in women's basketball.

In 1988 she toured with the Washington Generals, the team that traveled and played against the Harlem Globetrotters. The all-black, all-male Globetrotters, a team of skillful players, entertained fans with their humorous ball routines.

When the Women's National Basketball Association (WNBA) emerged in 1997, Lieberman suited up for the Phoenix Mercury. After a year of play, she coached the WNBA's Detroit Shock for three seasons. Then she pursued a career in broadcasting. With her high salary from the USBL and money from endorsements, broadcasting, and two instructional books she wrote, Lieberman became the first millionaire in women's

Ranking Women's Teams

Mel Greenberg, a journalist for the *Philadelphia Inquirer*, became a fan of women's basketball. In 1976 he started a weekly poll to determine the top 20 women's college teams. In 1978 the Associated Press continued to use Greenberg's ranking system, and the results are still printed in newspapers all over the country.

basketball. She credits Title IX for the opportunities given to women in sports and continues to promote women's professional basketball.

While the 1970s brought Title IX, the AIAW tournaments, better players, and more fans to women's basketball, the impact of television and newspaper coverage in the 1980s would bring more awareness and controversy at the college and professional levels.

Chapter 7

Off to College

After the enactment of Title IX, more women's athletic programs were created. However, most women's college programs were run by men. At that time, two associations governed the men's and women's athletic programs. The National Collegiate Athletic Association (NCAA) regulated the men's programs, while the AIAW oversaw the women's programs. The college directors preferred dealing with the NCAA because it had money and offered more incentives to athletes. They didn't like working with AIAW, because it resisted organizing national championship games and set restrictions on scholarships and academic requirements.

The NCAA started offering incentives to colleges to leave the AIAW and join the NCAA. Many athletic directors decided that having both their men's and women's programs governed by one set of rules would be easier. By 1982, 240 colleges had switched over to the NCAA. Not happy with these changes, the AIAW decided to file a lawsuit. They felt that the male-dominated NCAA did not focus on the welfare of female athletes and would ruin women's sports. The AIAW wanted to keep women's sports under the control of women, especially female coaches.

In 1982 the NCAA and the AIAW held tournaments on the same weekend. Seventeen of the top women's basketball teams played in the NCAA tournament. As thousands of fans watched, Louisiana Tech, coached by Sonya Hogg, beat Cheyney State, coached by C. Vivian Stringer. Louisiana Tech became the first NCAA women's championship team. CBS broadcast the game.

At the AIAW tournament, Rutgers grabbed the win from the University of Texas. Fearing competition with the CBS basketball telecast, NBC broke its contract with AIAW

C. Vivian Stringer

At Cheyney State University, C. Vivian Stringer taught her all-black women's basketball team innovative plays. She helped develop the Women's Basketball Coaches Association (WBCA) in 1981. In 1983 Stringer became head coach at the University of Iowa. In ten years she built a program that brought its Hawkeyes from obscurity to the Final Four.

In 1995, Stringer moved to Rutgers University in New Jersey. She received the highest salary of any U.S. women's basketball coach—$150,000 plus home care for her disabled daughter. Stringer brought her strengths of recruiting, discipline, and strategy to Rutgers. It paid off. In five years the Scarlet Knights reached the Final Four. This feat made Stringer the only basketball coach to take three different teams to the Final Four.

and did not televise the game. The AIAW tournament lost $8,800 and the AIAW lost their lawsuit. In June 1982, the AIAW dissolved its organization.

Cheryl Miller and the Beginning of the NCAA Era

The era of the NCAA tournaments had begun. During the season, teams played each other in four regional areas and three divisions. The winning teams from each region qualified for the NCAA tournaments, also called March Madness. The winners of the quarterfinals, known as the Sweet Sixteen, advanced to the Elite Eight. The remaining four winners played in the Final Four. In 1983 the NCAA contracted with ESPN to broadcast prechampionship games, with CBS airing the final game.

Now girls could see women playing basketball without leaving their homes. They sat by their TVs and watched 6-foot 2-inch Cheryl Miller, a freshman from the University of Southern California (USC), lead her team to a 69–67 victory against Louisiana Tech, the defending national champion. A dramatic player, Miller scored 27 points and fought

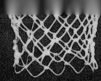

Cheryl Miller fights for possession of the ball while playing for the University of Southern California. She set nine USC records, including career scoring (3,018), rebounds (1,534), and steals (462).

A Better Basketball

In 1984 female players switched to a lighter, smaller ball.
Now they could pass faster and shoot better.

for the ball, making nine rebounds, four steals, and four blocks, and was awarded MVP.

Miller had set a California high school record by scoring 105 points in one game in 1982. Her moves were so smooth on the court she earned the nickname "Silk." More than 250 colleges offered her scholarships, but she chose USC.

In 1984, USC grabbed another championship by beating Tennessee, and Miller earned her second MVP. She broke NCAA women's tournament records for scoring, steals, and free throws. As a four-time Kodak All-American and three-time Naismith winner, Miller played in the 1984 Olympics. *Sports Illustrated* named her National Player of the Year in 1985.

In the late 1980s athletic departments started spending more money on women's sports. They began offering summer camps to high school girls. More men began coaching women's college sports. Schools chose men because they usually had more years of experience. By 1988 the NCAA had expanded to a 40-team tournament, and two years later it added eight more teams.

Coach Pat Summitt and UT

University of Tennessee (UT) coach Pat Summitt always ran an organized practice. She asked her players to think of other approaches when they made mistakes. She made her players scrimmage with men. Summitt required them to work out and study basketball films. She and her assistants carried cards listing drills and how long each drill should last. When one player didn't perform to expectations, the whole team had to run sprints.

Summitt's influence went further than the court. She required her players to sit within the first three rows in all their classes and finish all their assignments. If a player cut class, she wasn't allowed on the court. Most importantly, Summitt worked on self-esteem and respect.

At the 1987 NCAA Final Four, UT used amazing defense under Summit's guidance and defeated Louisiana Tech. In 1989, UT won its second NCAA Championship when they beat Auburn. During the 1991 NCAA championship game, the University of Virginia led by two points over UT with seven seconds remaining. Then Virginia's Dawn Staley fouled UT's Dena Head, who sank both free throws. With the score tied at 60, the game went into overtime—the first ever in an NCAA women's championship game. UT gained momentum and won 70–67.

Lady Volunteers' coach Pat Summitt holds up one of the basketball nets after her team won its third consecutive NCAA championship in 1998. Her son, Tyler, joins in the celebration.

One year before the 1996 Final Four, the 16,000 tickets were sold out within six hours. UT beat Georgia for the NCAA championship. In 1997, UT struggled during the season, but they reached the finals, playing against Old Dominion University. At halftime the Lady Vols led by 12 points. ODU fought back and gained a two-point lead. With seven minutes left, UT's Chamique Holdsclaw, a 6-foot 2-inch forward, exploded, scoring four baskets in a row. UT beat ODU for its second straight national championship. Holdsclaw was named MVP.

UT came back in 1998 hoping to be the first team to win three consecutive national championships. The Lady Vols walked onto the court with a 38–0 record to face Louisiana Tech. Thirteen minutes into the game, UT led 42–17 and never gave up. Winning 93–75, the Lady Vols grabbed their third consecutive NCAA title.

The Lady Vols ended the year 39–0, setting an NCAA record for most wins in a season for men's or women's basketball. This marked Pat Summitt's sixth NCAA tournament championship.

Chamique Holdsclaw became UT's all-time scorer with a 3,925-point record. She received the Broderick Cup and was chosen as the first female basketball player for the James E. Sullivan Memorial Award.

Ouch!

Sometimes Dawn Staley wears a rubber band on her right wrist. If she causes a turnover, she snaps the band to remind herself to shape up.

Shooting for 800

The very first team native-Texan Jody Conradt coached at Sam Houston State had a 15-4 record, and Conradt has racked up wins ever since. She became head coach at the University of Texas at Austin in 1976. On December 18, 1997, Conradt won her 700th game, making her the first women's basketball coach to do so. Near the end of the 2002 season, she had reached a record of 788 career wins (which was matched later that season by Pat Summitt).

Other Colleges Take the Title

There were years that Tennessee didn't win. In 1985, ODU beat Georgia, and Texas won over USC in 1986. Texas coach Jody Conradt encouraged her players to contribute input in setting standards for the team. Conradt's philosophy paid off. The win gave Texas a 34-0 record, making the Longhorns the first undefeated women's basketball team in the NCAA. In 1988, Coach Leon Barmore's Louisiana Tech beat Alabama at Auburn.

In the 1990 Final Four, Stanford University, led by point guard Jennifer Azzi, beat Auburn 88-81. Twenty thousand people attended. It was the first time attendance at a women's Final Four exceeded attendance at a men's Final Four game. Two years later, Stanford beat Western Kentucky to win its second championship in three years.

In an electrifying game, Texas Tech played against Ohio State at the 1993 finals. Texas Tech's Sheryl Swoopes proved to be a threat to Ohio. She was best known for her explosive first step to the basket and her three-point jump shots. During the game, Swoopes racked up a record 47 points, the most ever made in an NCAA final by either a male or a female player. She made all of 11 free throws. Texas Tech squeezed out an 84-82 victory.

Four months before the 1994 Final Four, tickets were sold out. In a game with Louisiana Tech up by two points, Charlotte Smith from the University of North Carolina released a three-point shot with less than a second left on the clock. Eleven thousand spectators held their breath. The ball dropped into the net as the buzzer sounded. North Carolina won 60–59. The one-point victory set a record. It was the first time a women's team had won an NCAA championship by one point.

In 1999, after three consecutive NCAA titles, UT didn't even make it to the Final Four. The last game of the NCAA championship matched Purdue against Duke. In the second half, Purdue's Ukari Figgs, who hadn't scored in the first half, brought victory to Purdue, earning her the MVP. Purdue rejoiced at their first NCAA title.

The 2001 NCAA finals pitted Purdue, the 1999 champions, against Notre Dame in St. Louis, Missouri. With less than two minutes to play, Purdue led 66–64. Then Ruth Riley, Notre Dame's 6-foot 5-inch center, tied it up. With more than a minute left, Riley was fouled. She sank the first free throw. Purdue called a time-out. Riley returned to the line and calmly sank her second shot.

The scoreboard read Notre Dame 68, Purdue 66. With 5.8 seconds left, the tension rose. Purdue's All-American Katie Douglas released an 18-footer. As the buzzer sounded, the ball hit the rim and bounced off the backboard. Notre Dame had won its first NCAA championship.

Coach Geno Auriemma and UConn

As a competitive coach, Geno Auriemma, of the University of Connecticut, does not necessarily pursue the best high school players. He believes a good team has chemistry, a blend of unselfish women who come together as a team to play their game. During some practices, Auriemma challenges his players by setting up tough situations, like making five players play against eight players. The five players have to figure out ways

Salary Struggles

In the early 1990s women's basketball coaches began demanding the same salaries as men's basketball coaches. In 1991, Coach Sanya Tyler, of Howard University in Washington, D.C., filed a lawsuit under Title IX, charging that she was paid less than the men's basketball coach and was not offered the job as athletic director. Tyler had an excellent team record for 11 years. The jury awarded her $2.4 million in 1993, but that amount was later reduced to $250,000. Then in 2000, Howard University fired Tyler for violation of university policies and NCAA regulations. Tyler has challenged those allegations with a lawsuit.

In 1993, USC coach Marianne Crawford Stanley tried to renegotiate her contract to receive the same pay as the USC men's coach. Before she came to USC in 1989, Stanley had won three championships for Old Dominion University (ODU) as a coach and two as a player for Immaculata. After negotiations fell apart, USC fired her, and Stanley filed an $8-million lawsuit, which she eventually lost. Then USC hired Cheryl Miller to replace her.

To finance her lawsuit, Stanley had to sell her home and use her savings. She had problems getting another coaching job. In the meantime, Stanley slept on a friend's couch and took low-paying jobs. At one point she had a job repairing furniture, but had to quit because her hands bled. When Stanford coach Tara VanDerveer took a leave of absence to coach the women's 1996 Olympic basketball team, Stanley replaced her for the year. Then in 1997, UC Berkeley hired Stanley to coach their women's basketball team. Stanley started coaching the WNBA's Washington Mystics in 2002.

to get around the extra defense players in order to shoot. This drill prepares them for tough situations in competitions.

In 1985, Auriemma hired Chris Dailey as associate head coach. Together they have fought to build a great women's basketball program at UConn. At that time, the facilities at UConn were second rate, and like most other schools, the women's team had to share the gym with the men's team. There was no media interest. Auriemma invited junior high and high school teams to fill the stands at Husky games, and he held clinics for high school coaches.

At the 1995 Final Four, UConn, with a 35–0 record, played UT, who had already won three NCAA titles. About 19,000 fans cheered at the arena, while 5.4 million viewers watched the game on TV. At halftime, UT led by six points, and three key UConn players sat on the bench with three fouls each.

With 12 minutes left to play and down by nine points, Husky Rebecca Lobo, a 6-foot 4-inch senior, hit four two-pointers, while the Vols didn't score. With 1 minute 51 seconds to go, Husky point guard Jennifer Rizzotti grabbed a rebound, outran two defenders, and made a left-handed layup to clinch the lead. Then Lobo, considered the best player in the nation, scored three free throws. UConn won its first NCAA championship, 70–64. The elated team carried Auriemma off the court.

When the Huskies returned home, 100,000 fans lined the streets to welcome them. The next day a photo of the team made the front page of *The New York Times*. That season the Huskies pulled in just under $900,000 from ticket sales and radio and television deals.

At the last game of the 2000 Final Four in Philadelphia, 20,060 fired-up fans shouted, "Go Huskies!" and "Go Lady Vols!" It was Auriemma's fourth Final Four with one national title and Summitt's twelfth Final Four with six national titles. The stage was set. The tension built. UT got off to a bad start. At the morning practice, Kristen "Ace"

UConn's Rebecca Lobo holds up the championship plaque and net after the Huskies beat the University of Tennessee in the 1995 finals.

Lobo a Celtic?

In fourth grade Rebecca Lobo wrote a letter to the president of the Boston Celtics, an NBA team. She told him she would be the first girl to play for the Celtics.

Clement had sprained her ankle and couldn't play. During the first 13 minutes of the game, the Huskies played aggressively, building a 21–6 lead. Tennessee's talented team never recovered. UConn hustled, grabbed the rebounds, and made steals to win 71–52.

During the 2002 Final Four, UConn arrived in San Antonio, Texas, with a 39–0 record to play against the University of Oklahoma, who came to the court with a 32–4 record. In 1990, Oklahoma had dropped its women's basketball program because of low attendance at games, which meant low income. Some students and parents were outraged and threatened to sue the university. The school reinstated the program within a week. In 1996, with a recommendation from Auriemma, Oklahoma hired Sherri Coale as

The Huskies lift Coach Geno Auriemma onto their shoulders after winning the championship against UT in 2000.

Geno Auriemma

Geno Auriemma immigrated to America from Italy at age seven. He made the basketball team in high school but mostly sat on the bench. Auriemma considers his high school coach, Buddy Gardler, one of his first role models.

When offered a job to coach high school girls in the mid-1970s, Auriemma's answer was, "No way. I wouldn't coach girls for all the money in the world." At that time he had preconceived ideas of what girls could and couldn't do as athletes. Finally, he took the job and coached the same way Buddy Gardler had coached him and his teammates. Auriemma learned that female players want what men want— to be challenged.

Off to the Snack Bar

According to officials at the First Union Center in Philadelphia, fans at the 2000 women's Final Four gobbled up 568 pounds of hot dogs, 840 pounds of steak, 2,564 minipizzas, and 2,769 pounds of French fries. They washed it all down with 3,173 gallons of soda. They also snacked on 16,536 pounds of popcorn, 5,955 soft pretzels, and 398 gallons of ice cream.

coach. That year she ended the season with a 5–22 record. Within six years, her Oklahoma Sooners were playing in the Final Four for the first time.

For inspiration during the season, the Sooners carried around a copy of *Sports Illustrated*, with 2002 gold medal skater Sarah Hughes on the cover. They also cut up a team photo into puzzle pieces. With each new success, a piece would be fitted into the puzzle. When the Sooners made it to the Final Four, all the pieces were in except for the middle piece, the one with Coach Sherri Coale on it.

During the second half of the final game, the Sooners trailed by 16. With less than three minutes left, the Sooners were only six points behind. But UConn executed their slick passing skills and out-rebounded the Sooners. In the end the Huskies won 82–70.

The Huskies had captured their third NCAA national title and second undefeated season. In honor of their win, Diana Taurasi threw the ball into the stands. Soon after the game, each Husky climbed the ladder to cut a string from the net—a basketball tradition.

UConn players on the bench erupt in celebration after capturing their third NCAA championship and their second undefeated season in 2002.

Chapter 8

Professionals and Olympians

Before the 1996 Olympics, the U.S. women's basketball team visited Washington, D.C. They had lunch with Representative Patsy Mink, a Democrat from Hawaii who supported the legislation for Title IX in 1972. She told the players—the Dream Team—that they weren't just earning the gold medal for themselves. They were winning it for thousands of girls who dreamed of being Olympians, too.

Early Professional Leagues

The popularity of women's basketball had increased greatly after the glory of the U.S. team winning the silver at the 1976 Olympics. Promoters and businesspeople felt the time was right for a professional women's league in the United States. They launched the Women's Professional Basketball League (WPBL) in 1978, headed by William Byrne, a former director of the defunct World Football League. Applications for franchises were sent out. Byrne contacted the Wilson Company, who agreed to supply basketballs for the new league.

Out of the 750 applications, eight franchises were chosen to form teams. The new owners of these franchises invested $50,000 each. Women were selected for the teams from top college senior players and free agents (those not in college or those under contract somewhere else). Some of the best players declined the WPBL's offers in order to keep their amateur status and be eligible for the 1980 Olympics. At that time any athlete who was paid to participate in a sport was considered a professional and could not compete in the Olympics.

The WPBL divided the league into four teams in the eastern division and four teams in the western division. Each team had a 34-game schedule and played 12-minute quarters, using a slightly smaller ball than the men's. On December 9, 1978, the first game matched the Chicago Hustle against the Milwaukee Does. Almost 8,000 people attended the game, which the Hustle won 92–87. Chicago station WGN-TV broadcast 10 of the Hustle's home games. About 1,200 fans attended each game.

Molly Bolin, the first WPBL pick, signed for $6,000. She had no experience playing the full-court game. Bolin had played half-court at her high school in Iowa. An excellent long-range jump shooter, she once scored 83 points in a single game. During the first year of the league, Bolin had played for the Iowa Cornets and averaged 16 points a game. By season three she boosted her average to 32.8 points per game. A sportswriter for *The Washington Post* nicknamed Bolin "Machine Gun Molly," because of her rapid-fire ability to score. She and her teammates traveled in a bus called the "Corn Dog." On one winter trip their game uniforms froze in the luggage compartment. Fortunately, they thawed out in time for the game.

Sometimes the games turned rough. Once when the New York Stars played against the Cornets, Stars player Althea Gwyn became annoyed at the way a Cornet player guarded her. Gwyn kept telling her to back off. Finally, Gwyn jammed her elbow into the player's ribs, knocking her down. The Cornet player lay unconscious for seven minutes.

The Cornets faced the Houston Angels for the final game of the 1979 playoffs. Nearly 6,000 fans packed the Hofheinz Pavilion in Texas. (During their home games, the Angels were used to playing in front of only 600 to 900 fans.) With two minutes to go, Angels player Paula "Moose" Mayo scored the last points to clinch the championship win, 111–104.

In season two, six new teams joined the league, now known as the Women's Basketball League (WBL). The WBL divided into three regional divisions. Bolin signed with the San Francisco Pioneers. Blond-haired, blue-eyed Bolin became the WBL promotional poster girl for women's basketball. She agreed with the WBL that posing in her short shorts would help bring fans to the games. That year the Stars won the championship against the Cornets.

Similar to prior leagues, the WBL wanted its players to be ladylike. The management for the New Orleans Pride hired makeup artists to help the players apply lipstick, eyeliner, and powder before each game. The California Dreams attended charm school and learned about good conversation, manners, and makeup.

In 1979 amateurs Ann Meyers, Carol Blazejowski, Nancy Lieberman, and Lusia Harris decided to join the WBL. These superstars gave a boost to the league. Lieberman asked for twice as much money as Meyers and got it. Blazejowski negotiated for three times as much as Meyers.

Problems with the Women's Basketball League

The WBL was doomed from the beginning. Its intentions were good, but its promotions and finances weren't. Players shifted from team to team, and teams moved to new cities with new names and new uniforms. The first All-Star game was taped, but never shown on TV. In a 1980 *Ebony* magazine article, some black WBL players complained that the WBL favored white women. Some people believed that the players were being exploited for their beauty and femininity, while others thought players were too masculine.

By now the investment to start a franchise had rocketed to $500,000. The WBL awarded Joseph Reither, a liquor store owner, the New England Gulls franchise. Reither drove a Cadillac and carried a lot of money. For Christmas he gave each of his players a $100 bill. Once he treated the Gulls to a fancy meal and paid their hotel room charges. But Reither mismanaged his finances and soon the players' paychecks bounced.

When the Gulls were scheduled to play against San Francisco in January 1981, they refused to suit up unless they got paid. Reither wanted them to sign statements saying that he wouldn't be held responsible for violating the WBL contract. He promised them they could split the ticket profits. The women refused his offer when they found out that they would have to pay for the officials and the use of the arena from their profits. The team got on the bus and went home.

Most teams lost at least $250,000. Some players didn't get paid, including Ann Meyers, who had signed a $130,000 three-year contract. Minnesota Fillies players who hadn't been paid walked out of a game in March 1981. Two teams never received their championship rings. Women lost their chance to play professionally the game they loved when the WBL closed down after three seasons.

More Leagues Come and Go

Before the WBL disbanded, the Ladies Professional Basketball Association, a six-team league, appeared in 1980. Three of the teams played just five games. The other three never played a single game. This league lasted less than a month.

In 1984, WBL founder William Byrne created another league called the Women's American Basketball Association (WABA). Nancy Lieberman signed a $250,000 contract with the Dallas Diamonds. Dallas won the championship title just before the WABA collapsed. Then came the National Women's Basketball Association in 1986. Its eight teams never played because the league dissolved before the season began.

Another pro league, called the Liberty Basketball Association (LBA), was formed with six teams in 1990. The women, wearing tight-fitting Spandex uniforms, shot at a basket only 9 feet 2 inches off the floor with a 25-inch ball. In an exhibition game on February 10, 1991, the Detroit Dazzlers beat the LBA All-Stars. This one and only game was played and televised in a stadium filled with nearly 11,000 spectators. Some believe it failed because of what the women wore and because they played on shorter courts with lower hoops.

Since pro leagues were not succeeding in the United States, dedicated female players joined basketball leagues in Europe and Asia. They earned good money, but spent a lot on phone calls and airline tickets. What these women wanted most was to play for U.S. fans.

A new six-team semipro league materialized in the Midwest in 1992. It scheduled a 15-game summer season for 1993. The league expanded by two teams in 1994 and regrouped and renamed some teams.

That year another league with eight teams sprouted—the Women's Basketball Association (WBA). Players earned $50 a game. The St. Louis River Queens faced the Chicago Twisters in the 1995 championship. Each Twister earned $75 for winning. After three seasons, the WBA ran out of money and folded. In 1997 plans for yet another league with 12 teams fizzled out.

American Basketball League

One day in February 1995 a trio of California parents held a meeting. Between them they had eight basketball-playing daughters, and they came to discuss organizing a women's basketball league. Gary Cavalli, a former athletic director at Stanford University, Anne Cribbs, a 1960 Olympic gold medal swimmer, and Steve Hams, a Palo Alto businessman, cofounded the American Basketball League (ABL).

Seven of the twelve 1996 U.S. Olympic players signed on with the ABL. The league also drafted top college players and American women who were playing international basketball. Another 570 women paid $200 apiece to try out. The league proposed a 40-game fall and winter schedule with an All-Star game and championship playoffs in March.

The first year the ABL operated with a $20 million budget. Players earned salaries ranging from $50,000 to $150,000. Reebok sponsored the games. Then the ABL

Shannon Johnson of the Columbus Quest goes up for a shot against the Richmond Rage during the 1997 season.

made a deal with Fox Sports-Net to televise up to 24 games. Black Entertainment Television agreed to broadcast 8 to 12 games.

The season opened October 18, 1996, with eight teams. Like the NBA, this league played with a 30-inch ball. Some ABL rules differed from NCAA women's rules. The ABL reduced the shot clock to 25 seconds, played 10-minute quarters, and allowed six fouls before benching players.

During the first ABL season, attendance averaged 3,500 fans a game. The Richmond Rage and the Columbus Quest made it to the 1997 playoffs. After four playoff games, the teams were tied. Then the Quest went on to win the championship in the fifth game.

For the second season the ABL added an expansion team in Long Beach, California. The *Long Beach Press-Telegram* held a contest called "Name That Team." Seventeen-year-old Todd Hunsacker created the winning name—Long Beach StingRays. Meanwhile, the Richmond Rage moved to Philadelphia and changed its name to the Philadelphia Rage. Four-time Olympian Teresa Edwards became the Atlanta Glory's player-coach. NBA Hall-of-Famer K. C. Jones took over as coach of the New England Blizzard.

Despite losing $4 million the first year, the ABL offered stock options to the players. Each player could earn money from the league's profits. Then the ABL secured contracts for more television coverage. They also signed 10 of the 13 most sought-after college players. Former Stanford guard and 1996 Olympian Jennifer Azzi signed a contract through the year 2000.

Attendance at the first game of the second season increased to 4,200. Ticket sales rose 80 percent. Reebok invested $15 million for a three-year period. In January of 1998, to recharge the fans, the ABL hosted an All-Star Weekend at Disney's Wide World of Sports complex in Florida. The FanFest weekend included a three-point shooting contest and an autograph session.

The highlight of the event was the first-ever women's slam-dunk contest. Sylvia Crawley, a 6-foot 5-inch Colorado Xplosion player, counted off 10 paces, put on a blindfold, saluted the crowd, exploded to the basket, and slam-dunked the ball. Shortly afterward, Crawley was traded to Portland in hopes of helping them move up from last place. The season closed with the defending champions, the Columbus Quest, winning their second title.

Before the third year, season ticket sales were up 30 percent, and the league expanded by two teams. CBS Sports signed a two-year agreement to broadcast two of the five playoff games. In hopes of breaking even or earning a profit, the ABL planned to add another team the following year.

However, some players and coaches chose to leave the league, a couple of top players made the injured list, and fewer top college players signed ABL contracts. Attendance dropped to 1,000 spectators at some arenas, forcing the StingRays and Atlanta Glory to fold. In an attempt to save the league, the advertising budget increased by $2 million. Soon the ABL was $10 million in debt and had to file for bankruptcy.

The ABL abruptly ceased operations on December 22, 1998. ABL co-founder Cavalli attributed the downfall to its rival league, the Women's National Basketball Association (WNBA). The NBA had created the WNBA in 1996 and ensured them sponsorship and plenty of television coverage.

The Olympics

More than 250 players tried out for the first U.S. women's Olympic basketball team in 1976. California State–Fullerton coach Billie Moore had only six weeks to prepare the all-collegiate U.S. team. They had to practice with boys' high school teams.

In game four of the Olympics in Montreal, Canada, the United States played the Soviet Union. The Soviets had Uljana Semjonova, who had never lost an international

Soviet player Uljana Semjonova was the first international player inducted into the Basketball Hall of Fame. She never lost a game in 18 years of international competition. Semjonova earned 15 gold medals from Soviet national championships, 11 from European championships, 3 from World Championships, and 2 from the Olympics.

competition. Because she was over 7 feet tall, *The New York Times* dubbed her the "Jolly Red Giant." Semjonova towered over Lusia Harris, the tallest U.S. player, by nearly a foot. Semjonova stood under the U.S. basket grabbing the rebounds. At her basket, she scored 32 points in 23 minutes, and the Soviets won 112–77. In their last game, the U.S. team beat Czechoslovakia and went home with silver medals, with Harris as the overall top U.S. scorer.

Pennies for Naismith

In 1936 the National Association of Basketball Coaches decided to send James Naismith, the inventor of basketball, to the Olympics in Berlin. Forty-three states held "Naismith Nights" basketball games. The association collected a penny from every ticket sold, and this totaled almost $5,000. In Berlin, Naismith tossed up the ball for the first Olympic men's basketball game. United States and Canada played the championship game outdoors in a rainstorm. During one U.S. play, the ball got stuck in the mud, but the United States won the gold medal.

In 1979, when the Soviet Union invaded Afghanistan, President Jimmy Carter mandated U.S. athletes to boycott, or not participate in, the 1980 Olympics in Moscow. The Soviet women's basketball team won the gold on its home court.

The 1984 Olympics were held in Los Angeles. To retaliate for the U.S. boycott of the 1980 Olympics, the Soviet Union boycotted the 1984 Olympics. The University of Tennessee coach Pat Summitt, who had played in the 1976 Olympics, coached the U.S. women's team. Among the Olympic players was ODU's 6-foot 7-inch Anne Donovan. Her outstanding skills in high school made Donovan the most sought-after college recruit. She could go out for the fast break and shoot, then turn around and rush back in time to defend her basket. Donovan could also shoot from the outside, and she had a mean hook shot. At ODU, she set 15 school records and played in two national championships. Donovan, a three-time All-American, was the first female Naismith Trophy winner.

Another choice for the 1984 team was Lynette Woodard. While at the University of Kansas, she had racked up 3,649 points, and she led the nation in steals. Woodard was a four-time Kodak All-American. Rounding out the roster were UCLA's Denise Curry,

Georgia's Teresa Edwards, and USC's Cheryl Miller and Pamela McGee. The team breezed through the round-robin competition and beat Korea to capture the gold. Miller scored more than any other player.

The Soviets returned to the Olympics for the 1988 games in Seoul, South Korea, without the 7-foot Uljana Semjonova. She retired from basketball in 1986 because she couldn't keep up with the faster game. North Carolina State coach Kay Yow coached the U.S. team. Olympic veterans Donovan and Edwards returned. Miller could not play because of a knee injury. An Olympic committee chose USC's Cynthia Cooper, Penn State's Suzie McConnell, Louisiana Tech's Teresa Weatherspoon, Maryland's Vicky Bullett, Mississippi's Jennifer Gillom, and Georgia's Katrina McClain.

More than half of the dozen members had played on an overseas team and had experience competing at the Goodwill Games and World Championships. In the Olympic finals against Yugoslavia, Edwards's outside shots and Weatherspoon's and McConnell's lightning-quick plays led the United States to a 77–70 win for the gold. The Soviets went home with the bronze.

In 1992 professional players were allowed to compete in the Olympics. Six players from the 1988 U.S. Olympic team were selected to play at the 1992 games held in Barcelona, Spain. Rutgers's Theresa Shank Grentz coached the team. In the semifinals the United States faced the Unified Team, which replaced that of the former Soviet Union. The Unified Team had a new game plan. A Unified player threw the inbound pass to a tall teammate, who passed it up court to a quick guard. This passing play cut the length of the court and gave the guard more time to shoot.

The United States fell apart. Point guard McConnell made costly turnovers. Edwards and McClain shot poorly. The Unified Team won 79–73 and went on to earn the gold after defeating China. The U.S. team played Cuba and ended up with the bronze.

The 1996 Olympic committee picked Stanford coach Tara VanDerveer to coach the

U.S. women's team. Unhappy that most players had already been selected through the committee, VanDerveer questioned the choices of Rebecca Lobo and former UT player Nikki McCray because of their lack of international experience. She was also worried that Edwards and McClain weren't team players.

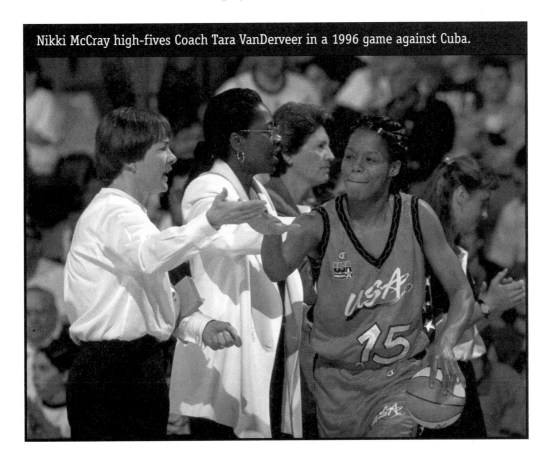

Nikki McCray high-fives Coach Tara VanDerveer in a 1996 game against Cuba.

To build their strength, Coach VanDerveer put the team through weight training and hours and hours of running. The players practiced drills and trust exercises. They scrimmaged with men's teams. They watched basketball videos, learned strategies, and took notes. VanDerveer gave out fines to players who wore the wrong socks or headbands. When Lobo, who had a contract with Reebok, forgot her shoes, VanDerveer made Lobo wear Ruthie Bolton's Nikes.

USA Basketball

An organization called USA Basketball invested $3 million to support the 1996 women's Olympic team. This organization is the National Sports Governing Body within the U.S. Olympic Committee. It is affiliated with the AAU, the NBA, the NCAA, and others. Sponsors like Nike, Sears, State Farm Insurance, and Lifetime TV came up with $6 million to finance the team's training and traveling expenses.

The U.S. team played 52 exhibition games before the Olympics. At one of these games McCray's boyfriend proposed marriage to her in front of 6,000 spectators. She accepted. When the team visited the Supreme Court in Washington, D.C., Justices Sandra Day O'Connor and Ruth Bader Ginsburg took them up to the third floor to see the basketball court. Then the two justices shot baskets with the Dream Team.

Before the games began in Atlanta, the team not only visualized standing on the podium accepting gold medals, but also practiced it. During the quarterfinals, former USC player Lisa Leslie scored 35 points against Japan, setting a U.S. record. In the final game every player scored at least two points. The United States beat Brazil 111–87 to win the gold with a 60–0 record. After the buzzer the Dream Team turned cartwheels and danced all over the court.

The 2000 U.S. Olympic team was made up of professional players from the Women's National Basketball Association (WNBA), formed in 1997. Just after the close of the summer season, they flew to Sydney, Australia. During the games, U.S. coach Nell Fortner stressed defense.

The 1996 Dream Team stands for the U.S. National Anthem during the Olympic medal ceremony. Gold medalists from left to right are: Jennifer Azzi, Lisa Leslie, Carla McGhee, Katy Steding, Katrina McClain, Rebecca Lobo, Venus Lacy, and Nikki McCray.

The U.S. team dominated Australia during its final game. Los Angeles Sparks player Lisa Leslie and Utah Starzz player Natalie Williams each scored 15 points and collected 9 rebounds for the U.S. team. Houston Comet Sheryl Swoopes contributed 14 points and 9 rebounds. Sacramento Monarch Yolanda Griffith added 13 points and 12 rebounds. Despite these great numbers, Australia's Lauren Jackson, a 19-year-old center, led the game with 20 points, 13 rebounds, and 3 blocks. The United States beat Australia, 76–54.

Near the end of the game, Leslie's hair extension fell off. She scooped it up and tossed it into the photographers' section. Leslie was heard saying that the photographers could have her hair because her team won the gold.

Olympic Coaches Corner

1976, Billie Moore—silver

In the 1950s there were no sports for girls at the high school in Topeka, Kansas, that Billie Moore attended. That didn't stop her. She became a star third baseman with the Ohse Meats, a nationally known women's fast-pitch softball team in Topeka.

As a basketball coach, Moore won national championships at two schools, California State–Fullerton in 1970 and UCLA in 1978 with Ann Meyers and Denise Curry on the team. In the early 1970s she coached U.S. teams in the World University and Pan American games. She assisted in the selection of every major U.S. international team from 1976 until her retirement.

1980, Boycotted

1984, Pat Summitt—gold

Pat Head Summitt played basketball with her three older brothers in the hayloft of their dairy farm. She grew up in an organized household where work was expected and not praised. Before making the 1976 Olympic team, she trained six hours a day, regained strength in an injured knee, and lost weight.

Not much seems to faze her. After a recruiting trip to Pennsylvania in September 1990, a pregnant Summitt experienced a bumpy, stressful plane trip back home. Within hours she went into labor and gave birth to a son.

Summitt was the first women's coach to be on the cover of *Sports Illustrated*. At the end of the 2002 season, she tied Jody Conradt's record of 788 career wins. One of the highest paid women's coaches, Summitt has signed a contract through 2005 with a $550,000 package.

1988, Kay Yow—gold

As a coach at North Carolina State for 27 years, Kay Yow has led her teams to over 600 wins. She credits her staff, players, and managers for the great basketball program at N.C. State. In 1986 she coached the U.S. team to gold at the Goodwill Games and the World Championships.

In 2002 the Raleigh, North Carolina, mayor proclaimed February 13th "Kay Yow Day." The Raleigh 7-Up bottler locally distributed 7-Up cans with Yow's image on them. The Yow coaching legacy continues with her two sisters, who have coached at the college level.

1992, Theresa Shank Grentz—bronze

Theresa Shank Grentz played basketball with the boys in Glenolden, Pennsylvania. As a Mighty Mac player at Immaculata, she sold candy bars to pay for travel expenses. The Macs won three AIAW championships. In 1976, Rutgers in New Jersey hired Grentz, making her the first full-time women's basketball coach. Her 1982 Rutgers team won the AIAW championship. Like her coach, Cathy Rush, Grentz demands a disciplined practice from her players, and is now at the University of Illinois at Champaign-Urbana.

1996, Tara VanDerveer—gold

Tara VanDerveer has always treasured an old newspaper clipping about her grandfather playing basketball for the Baltimore & Ohio Railroad team in the 1920s. The article says that with seconds left to play, he made a basket and two free throws to win the game.

On her first day of college at SUNY–Albany in New York, she headed to the gym for pickup games with the guys. Not satisfied with her basketball team, VanDerveer drove to Illinois to watch the 1972 AIAW championships and find a new school with a better team. She liked Indiana University's team and transferred there. VanDerveer often went to watch and learn coaching techniques from Bobby Knight, Indiana's men's coach.

2000, Nell Fortner—gold

While at the University of Texas, Nell Fortner competed in volleyball. She also played basketball under Coach Jody Conradt. Fortner first coached at Killeen High School in Texas. She credits her brother, coaches Leon Barmore and Pat Summitt, and players Blazejowski and Meyers as her role models. After being the assistant coach for the 1996 Olympics, Fortner became head coach for Purdue University in Indiana. Then USA Basketball appointed her the head coach for the USA Basketball Women's National Team Program in 1997. Fortner became head coach for the WNBA's Indiana Fever in 2001.

Fortner has a positive and encouraging coaching style. She teaches as she coaches because she believes there's always something to learn about the game. Fortner feels that having a winning attitude is the best place to start. A workaholic, Fortner sets big expectations and works hard to meet them.

Chapter 9

We Got Game: The WNBA

To inspire girls, the women's basketball pro leagues created slogans. The American Basketball League players said, "Little girls need big girls to look up to." The Women's National Basketball Association players shouted, "We got next!" That term was first used on playgrounds, and it meant that one group of players was waiting to take on the winners. Later, the WNBA's official slogan became, "We Got Game."

Creating the WNBA

The WNBA announced that their league would begin play in June 1997. Eight teams, four each in the Eastern and Western Conferences, would play a three-month summer season. On January 22, 1997, the WNBA assigned 16 top players to the teams. In April, the WNBA team coaches drafted another 16 players. Coach Van Chancellor, who would coach the Houston Comets, drew the first pick, USC forward Tina Thompson. Carol Blazejowski, a Naismith Hall of Fame inductee, became vice president and general manager of the New York Liberty.

The WNBA then announced tryouts for the remaining spots on each team. Four teams had nearly 250 women try out in each of their cities. The hopefuls ranged from a 50-year-old grandmother to an Olympic medalist from overseas. Katasha Artis from Northeastern University in Boston rode 14 hours on a bus to the Charlotte, North Carolina, tryouts. Her dream came true, and she became a WNBA basketball player.

WNBA president Val Ackerman was a four-year starter at the University of Virginia in the late 1970s and early 1980s. She and her staff chose the WNBA logo from an assortment of 50 designs. Then fashion designers sketched various styles of uniforms—

one of them was even a dress! On May 21, 1997, the uniforms were presented to the public: three jerseys and two shorts silhouettes.

Today players wear jerseys made of rayon, nylon, or polyester fabric. The jerseys are lightweight with tiny holes to let air circulate. Each jersey has the team name and player's number on the front and the player's last name and number on the back. Long, loose fitting boxer shorts are made of the same fabric as the jerseys. Most players wear bicycle pants under their baggy shorts. Uniforms are one solid color with other colors for trim. During home games, teams wear light-colored uniforms, and for road games they wear dark uniforms.

For protection, players wear pads, goggles, and mouth guards. Pads protect the knees and elbows and cushion them when a player falls. Some players wear goggles to protect their glasses and eyes from other players' fingers or elbows. Mouth guards fit over the teeth for protection and come in different colors.

Spalding created balls of different designs and colors so the WNBA staff could choose the official ball. When the balls were delivered, the paint on them was still wet. As the staff tested the balls, splotches of paint stuck to the floor. It had to be cleaned in time for an afternoon NBA game. The staff chose an orange-and-oatmeal colored ball, because when it spun through the air it looked like a pinwheel.

The WNBA followed college regulations. The lanes of the court measured 12 feet wide and the distance for three-point shots measured 19 feet 9 inches from the basket. Basic rules included a 28.5-inch ball, a 30-second shot clock, and two 20-minute halves.

The 1997 starting salaries ranged from $15,000 to $50,000. The first draft picks earned the higher salaries. The league also offered housing and other bonuses. Players had to be 21 years old or have completed their college eligibility.

The NBA and the WNBA decided to have the same mascot and colors for their teams at shared cities. The Utah Starzz shared the double z with their NBA Jazz

Fashion Statements

- Pro players don't have to wear makeup or worry about their hair as the Red Heads did. But Tina Thompson of the Houston Comets always wears deep red lipstick because she feels it brought her good luck during her first college game.

- Teresa Weatherspoon, point guard for the New York Liberty, wears jersey number 11. "Spoon" picked number 11 to honor her favorite uncle, who died when she was 11 years old. Spoon also wears 11 braids in her hair.

- Michele Timms, former point guard for the Phoenix Mercury, wore a new pair of socks for each game. She owns socks from all over the world. One time by mistake, Nike sent her 70 pairs!

- Sheryl Swoopes of the Houston Comets was the first woman ever to have a basketball shoe created and named for her: "Air Swoopes." Rebecca Lobo was next to have shoes named after her. LA Sparks' Lisa Leslie, who wears jersey number 9, has shoes named after her number, "Total Air 9." Tina Thompson's shoes were called "Air Post 'Em Up."

- To pump herself up before a game, Chamique Holdsclaw of the Washington Mystics writes inspirational messages like "Don't dream it. Be it." on her size 15 shoes.

counterparts. When the deadline approached for the Los Angeles team to come up with their name, Johnny Buss, president of the team, had nothing. While Buss was on the phone talking with the WNBA, his assistant, Brandi Bratcher, was on another line with her father discussing team names. Her father, a welder, suggested the name "Sparks," because sparks fly when someone is welding, and this LA team was going to fly, too.

WNBA Tip-off

The first WNBA game took place at the Great Western Forum in Inglewood, California, on June 21, 1997. Ackerman tossed the jump ball between the Los Angeles Sparks's Lisa Leslie and the New York Liberty's Kym Hampton. When Penny Toler, a Sparks guard, sank the first basket, over 14,000 fans cheered. The Liberty won, 67–57. Two days later, the Sparks played against the Utah Starzz. The Starzz won 102–89, making it the WNBA's first 100-point game.

At the beginning of the season, most teams played poorly. Three weeks of practice hadn't been enough time to bring the teams together. But the fans stuck by them, and the teams began to jell. At one Charlotte Sting game nearly 19,000 people attended. On average, 9,500 fans filled the arenas at each game that first season.

Before each game, the WNBA players presented basketballs to a select group of local children. This ball presentation became a tradition. After the games, the tired and sweaty players signed autographs and posed for pictures. The devoted fans connected with their teams and kept coming back. WNBA games became a fun and inexpensive family outing.

During the first season, Houston Comets star player Sheryl Swoopes went on maternity leave. The Comets decided they needed new energy. Coach Van Chancellor encouraged Cynthia Cooper to step up to the challenge. "Coop" did just that and broke the league's scoring record three times in one week. Coop pumped her arms in the air

Kisha Ford of the New York Liberty tries to pass the ball against the Los Angeles Sparks during the very first WNBA game on June 21, 1997.

after scoring to get the fans to "raise the roof." This became her trademark. The fans mimicked her and cheered. After Swoopes returned, the team won enough games to go to the playoffs. On August 30, 1997, the first WNBA Championship game was televised in 165 countries. The Comets won 65–51 over the Liberty.

By the second season the WNBA added teams in Detroit and Washington, D.C. The Comets took the championship again. Two more teams, the Orlando Miracle and the Minnesota Lynx, joined the league in 1999. That season featured the first WNBA All-Star game.

One of the highlights of the 1999 season came during the second game of the championship round in the playoffs. The Liberty was trailing the Comets when Liberty point guard Teresa Weatherspoon got possession of the ball with seconds left to play. At about 50 feet from the basket, "Spoon" released the ball and hit the shot. She fell on her knees in disbelief. Her team still had a chance at the title. But the Liberty lost the third game, and the Comets grabbed the title for the third time. Coach Chancellor earned his third WNBA Coach of the Year award.

Ticket, Please

In 1999 former U.S. Senator Birch Bayh of Indiana, one of the authors of Title IX, continued to show his support for women's sports when he bought the 5,500th ticket for the 2000 season of the Indiana Fever.

The league increased to 16 teams and a 32-game schedule in 2000. The Comets won their fourth championship, and Cynthia Cooper earned her fourth playoff MVP trophy. She retired as a player and became the coach of the Phoenix Mercury.

In 2001 the Comets were knocked out of the playoffs during the first round. The Sparks faced the Sting for the championship. The Sting started the season with a 1–10 record but turned around by season's end with 22–18. The Sparks entered the playoffs with a 34–5 record. At the beginning of the final game, the Sparks missed shots, made turnovers, and fell behind. Then Sting's Allison Feaster, a former LA Spark, scored seven points. Sparks player Mwadi Mabika answered by knocking down some three-pointers of her own.

Then the Sparks got game. Lisa Leslie scored 24 points, grabbed 13 rebounds, dished out 6 assists, and blocked 7 shots. The Sparks won the 2001 championship, 82–54. This victory marked the largest point difference of a championship playoff game in the history of the WNBA.

Leslie was unanimously voted MVP of the playoffs. She became the first WNBA player to earn MVP at the All-Star game, the regular season, and the playoffs. Leslie praised Coach Michael Cooper for bringing the Sparks to a higher level. Cooper, who had won five NBA titles as a player with the Los Angeles Lakers in the 1980s, acknowledges the WNBA championship as one of his best achievements.

As the league headed into its sixth season, it was faced with drops in attendance, the reality of not turning a profit, and concerns from its players that the $12 million payroll is unfairly distributed. Nevertheless, no other women's league with teams nationwide lasted this long. In time, the league hopes to establish teams in every one of the 29 NBA cities.

LA Sparks' Lisa Leslie grabs the rebound over Charlotte Sting's Tammy Sutton-Brown during the 2001 WNBA finals. The Sparks went on to win the championship, and Leslie was voted MVP of the playoffs. The following season, she became the first player to dunk the ball in a WNBA game.

High Five! 2002 Top Draft Picks

Giving each other high fives may be just what the University of Connecticut's fabulous five starters did after they won the 2002 NCAA championship. Four of the five Huskies graduated to the WNBA, while 6-foot sophomore Diana Taurasi, an excellent shooting guard, remained at UConn.

Not only did Sue Bird, Swin Cash, Asjha Jones, and Tamika Williams play UConn basketball together and receive NCAA championship rings for 2000 and 2002, they also roomed together and made the Dean's List. The girls even prepared dinner together once a week. Williams, a 6-foot 2-inch defender, cooked the meat dish. Cash, a 6-foot 2-inch forward, made the side dish. Jones, another 6-foot 2-inch forward, cooked pasta. And Bird, a 5-foot 9-inch point guard, prepared dessert. Sometimes she bought four pints of Ben & Jerry's ice cream, one for each roommate. These former Huskies have now gone their separate ways. They are professional basketball players for the WNBA.

Stacey Dales, a 6-foot University of Oklahoma guard and a 2000 Canadian Olympian, posed a threat to UConn during the 2002 NCAA championship. Two weeks after the Final Four, she got a ring, too—a wedding ring—and became Mrs. Dales-Schuman.

2002 First Round Draft Picks

Pick 1: Sue Bird to the Seattle Storm

Pick 2: Swin Cash to the Detroit Shock

Pick 3: Stacey Dales-Schuman to the Washington Mystics

Pick 4: Asjha Jones to the Washington Mystics

Pick 5: Nikki Teasley to the Portland Fire, then traded to the LA Sparks

Pick 6: Tamika Williams to the Minnesota Lynx

Chapter 10

In the Hall

Hundreds of people gathered in downtown Knoxville, Tennessee, for the ceremonial bricklaying for the Women's Basketball Hall of Fame (WBHOF) on April 9, 1998. Betty Jaynes, executive director of the Women's Basketball Coaches Association (WBCA), and Barbara Dietz, a $100,000 contributor, placed the first two of the 300 bricks to be laid that day. Brick masons added mortar to seal them into the wall. Then each member of the women's U.S. national team added a brick. Fans waited behind them in a long line, holding their bricks. Many of them were young girls. Perhaps some of them will become basketball players inducted into the Hall of Fame.

The Dream

The idea for the WBHOF started with Michael Gillespie, a minister and sports announcer in Jackson, Tennessee. In 1991, Phyllis Holmes, former official of the National Association of Intercollegiate Athletics, presented the idea to the coaches at the WBCA. Their board of directors started raising money to build the Hall in Jackson. But after three years, the board hadn't raised enough money. They decided to pick a better location that would inspire more donations and draw more tourists.

In 1996, Gloria Ray, president of Knoxville Sports Corporation, threw herself into the project. Pat Summitt, a WBHOF board member, actively helped raise money for the hall. Soon other businesses from east Tennessee made donations. The Knoxville City Council, Eastman Chemical Company, and the state of Tennessee gave nearly $3 million. Other contributions came from 40 states. Local business executive Pete DeBusk donated the half-million-dollar, 2.2-acre site. The cost of the entire project totaled more than $9 million.

Bullock, Smith, and Partners designed the 32,000-square foot glass and concrete building. Valerie Key, project manager for 1220 Exhibits Inc., made phone calls, wrote letters, and traveled around the country to collect artifacts and mementos for the hall. Patsy Neal, a former Flying Queen, sorted through her old trunks and suitcases. She contributed nearly 100 items. Another large collection came from Alline Banks Sprouse, an 11-time AAU All-American during the 1940s.

The three-day WBHOF's grand opening started with a WNBA exhibition game at Thompson-Boling Arena in Knoxville. The next evening a bronze statue of three female basketball players was unveiled at the Hall. Then on June 5, 1999, the doors opened and visitors took their first look at 107 years of women's basketball history. That evening the gala ended with the induction ceremony of the class of 1999.

A Tour of the Hall of Fame

Visitors enter the WBHOF on the upper floor. A larger-than-life sculpture dominates the two-floor open atrium. Artist Elizabeth MacQueen sculpted the 17-foot-high piece, titled *Honor the Past; Celebrate the Present; Promote the Future*, which is the mission statement of the WBHOF.

The sculpture includes a figure of a woman passing the ball, dressed in the middie blouse and bloomers of players from the past. A second woman shooting the ball represents the present. She wears an Olympic USA Basketball uniform in honor of five-time Olympian Teresa Edwards. A third figure of a young girl dribbling a basketball promotes the future. Money from Eastman Chemical Company paid for the sculpture, which is welded onto a 20-foot steel pedestal. Each inductee into the Hall of Fame receives an Eastman Award, which is a small version of the main sculpture.

Visitors to the WBHOF are ushered into a small theater to watch a video titled "Hoopful of Hope." It's packed with more than 100 years of basketball history, including

The Women's Basketball Hall of Fame in Knoxville, Tennessee

footage of women playing in the early 1900s. It shows famous players of the past and present, including the Red Heads in action. There's even a sequence of blindfolded Sylvia Crawley dunking the ball.

The first major display, titled "The First 100 Years," fills an entire wall. (Keep in mind that some displays in the Hall will change over the years.) On the far right, there's a copy of Senda Berenson's notice prohibiting men from entering the gym. In the photos from the year 1947, you can see that players started wearing their numbers on both the front and back of their uniforms. (From 1927 until 1947 players wore their numbers only on the back.) There are history questions on the ledge of the 100-year timeline. You can turn over the basketballs next to each question to check your answers.

The next area has a lifelike animatronic figure of Senda Berenson, "Mother of Women's Basketball," and her students at Smith College. They are dressed in middie blouses and wool bloomers. Berenson explains how the game was played in the late 1890s and early 1900s. Across from this exhibit is a replica of a women's locker room from the early 1900s. The women had to share the space under the stairs of the gym with

Giant Basketball

A 30-foot-wide basketball, the Báden Ball, dominates the top of the WBHOF building. Báden is a brand name of a company that manufactures athletic balls. The ball was shipped from Minnesota in eight sections. Once it reached Knoxville, it was assembled and painted. A crane hoisted the ball onto the steel net. The ball weighs 20,000 pounds. Its surface is fiberglass, with 96,000 "nubs," or pebbles, that make it look real.

a custodian's supplies. On the video in the center of the room, coaches and players talk about how tough it was for women to get money, equipment, uniforms, gym time, and scholarships. It's clear that these women pioneers kept playing because of their love for the game.

In the AAU Feature Case are Maxine Vaughn's 1944 tournament beauty queen cup and her 1947 AAU free throw championship trophy. In 1951, Vaughn, a two-time All-American, led the Hanes Hosiery team to an AAU championship. The team's 2-foot trophy also stands in the case. Two jackets hang inside. They belong to Flying Queen Patsy Neal and Hanes player Eckie Jordan.

The sculpture that adorns the lobby of the Hall of Fame

Double glass cases feature eight-time All-American Margaret Sexton Gleaves's warm-up jacket from when she played for Cook's Goldblumes. Also displayed are the leather sheepskin-lined kneepads players wore during the 1940s, and the GymKing sneakers that were popular sports shoes in the 1940s and 1950s. There are even a 1947 Iowa Girl's Basketball Scrapbook and some souvenir programs that originally cost up to 25 cents.

The next area is called the "Modern Locker Room." You can sit next to a life-sized model of a player and watch a video of coaches talking to their teams, giving them encouragement, and working out plays on a chalkboard. There are replicas of college and U.S.A. national team players' lockers. They are filled with uniforms, shoes, posters, basketballs, trophies, trading cards, and lots more.

In the upper deck there's a circular glass case called the "Players of the Year." The four jerseys belong to the high school and college players of the year, the USA Basketball female athlete of the year, and the WNBA MVP. Each player's statistics are featured.

One of the historic display cases in the Women's Basketball Hall of Fame

More than 140 jerseys from current high school and college All-Americans and WNBA All-Stars hang from the rafters. This area is called the "Ring of Honor." A holder on the wall contains lists of the names of the athletes who wore the jerseys.

Sets of International Basketball cases feature items from the World Championships, Pan American games, and the Olympics. The jacket that Anne Donovan wore when she played for a professional team in Japan, as well as Sheryl Swoopes's shoes, are displayed. The balls are autographed by the U.S. Olympic teams.

The "Players, Coaches & Programs" area has two sets of cases. The first set honors coaches Jody Conradt and Pat Summitt, who belong to the elite group of women who have each coached over 700 winning games. The second set of cases has a blue WBL New England Gulls shirt and a photo of the Macs wearing short skirts and bib apron tops over their white shirts. Coca-Cola bottles on display were designed especially for Louisiana Tech's 1981 AIAW national championship. There are also jewelry and a national championship ring that belonged to Holly Warlick, former UT point guard, who has been Summitt's assistant coach since 1985. Another case holds current posters, tickets, jerseys, and souvenir balls from Final Four games.

At the "Official's Wall," information is displayed about Darlene May, the first female to referee a women's Olympic basketball game in 1984, and Violet Palmer and Dee Kantner, who were the first women to officiate at a men's NBA game, in 1997.

The hall also exhibits the 1966 white limousine that transported the All American Red Heads across the country. On the wall are posters and several red-and-white striped Red Heads' jerseys. A double glass case holds many Red Heads' items, such as their white basketball, which was luminescent and glowed in the dark under black lights. (Imagine it flying across the court during their half-time routines!) The Red Heads also dazzled their fans with a red, white, and blue traveling trunk, sequined top hat, and large fake glasses, which are all on display. Red-and-white-striped knee-high socks that are shown were standard wear for the Red Heads.

In an area called "In the Huddle," there are four life-sized statues of women players listening to coaches during time-outs. At "I'm in the Hall," across from the huddle, you can fill out a form on the computer screen and have your picture taken. The picture is later uploaded to The Hall of Fame's Web site, www.WBHOF.com.

The last room is called the "State Farm Hall of Honor." It contains photos of the inductees and information about them. Two oval cases display memorabilia from some of the inductees.

A lower level, called the "Athletic Playground," has eight interactive games. You can shoot baskets at all three courts. The directions are posted on the wall. You can measure your jump at the Vertical Leap panel, and you can practice dribbling on the courses painted on the floor.

Induction Production

Before being inducted, a person must be nominated as a player, coach, referee, or contributor. The WBHOF Board of Directors serves as a selection committee. They consider statistics, letters of recommendation, and the nominee's contribution to basketball. To be eligible:

- Players must be retired from their highest level of play for five years.
- Coaches must have coached women's games for at least 20 years.
- Referees must have officiated at women's games for a minimum of ten years.
- Contributors must make a significant impact on the women's game.

Outside at the front of the WBHOF building, names of teams, players, coaches, and fans are engraved on the bricks that form the shape of a giant basketball embedded in the ground.

Naismith Memorial Basketball Hall of Fame

Before the WBHOF, there was the Naismith Memorial Basketball Hall of Fame. In 1949 it was in a little red house next to the football field at Springfield College in Massachusetts. The National Association of Basketball Coaches (NABC) decided to raise funds to construct a new building. They started to collect basketball artifacts and to induct male players, coaches, contributors, referees, and teams. The Hall finally opened on February 17, 1968.

After ten years there wasn't enough room for additional exhibits. Plans for a three-level building began. Then on June 30, 1985, a second Hall of Fame opened in downtown Springfield. That year the Hall started inducting women and showcasing their history. As of 2002, about 8 percent of the more than 200 inductees are women.

The second Hall lasted 17 years. In the fall of 2002, a $103-million complex replaced the 1985 building. In its center stands a state-of-the-art, three-tiered, 60,000-square-foot Hall, nearly double the size of the previous building. The complex has a promenade with a basketball-themed restaurant and stores.

When you enter the lobby, it feels as if you're in a real basketball arena. The focal point of the Hall is the huge Center Court. Three levels surround the sides of the dome-shaped building. The top tier showcases the theme "many faces, one game" in its Honors Ring. Glass plaque portraits of the more than 200 enshrined male and female players, coaches, and teams wrap around the dome. On the bottom level you can play on a full-size basketball court, pick a skill activity, or answer trivia questions.

The second level exhibits interactive displays and the chronological history of basketball. At "The Game" area, there are artifacts and graphics about barnstorming teams, international games, and basketball inventor James Naismith. Theatrical sets at "The Players" area recreate rural, suburban, and urban basketball courts. The "Contributors to the Game" area features referees. Basketball plays are shown on a video, and visitors can have their picture taken with a team mascot.

The Past, the Present, and the Future

The title of the bronze statue in the WBHOF sums up the history of women's basketball: "Honor the Past; Celebrate the Present; Promote the Future."

• Honor the Past: Many girls and women have benefited from Title IX and more than 100 years of talent, drive, innovation, and love for basketball, as shown by the women and men before them.

• Celebrate the Present: Players and coaches of today are passing on what they have learned, their passion for the game, and the importance of hard work, respect, and setting goals for the future.

• Promote the Future: Tomorrow's girls and women will carry on these legacies and the ball into the next generation.

Class of 2006!

Top high school girls' basketball players send videotapes of their best games to college coaches, along with a letter listing their personal and basketball statistics. Some visit the college. The following players, who were highly sought after by college coaches, are on their way to four years of great college basketball:

- Seimone Augustus, a 6-foot 1-inch guard/forward, signed with Louisiana State on her birthday. She can score from midrange, slam-dunk the ball, and handle the ball with skill.
- Willnett Crockett, a 6-foot 3-inch center/forward, signed with UConn. She is a scoring machine and defends with intimidation.
- Lindsay Richards, a 5-foot 8-inch point guard, signed with Iowa. She is a great leader and can shoot and pass well.
- Ann Strother, a 6-foot 1-inch versatile guard and Naismith High School Player of the Year, signed with UConn. She was a starter on the Junior World Championship team.
- Nicole Wolff, a 5-foot 11-inch guard, signed with UConn. She can shoot from anywhere and makes good decisions on the court.
- Shanna Zolman, a 5-foot 9-inch center, signed with UT. She makes 90 percent of her free throws and hits more than 50 percent of her three-pointers. She is considered a complete player and a scoring machine.

Appendix 1
Women's Professional Basketball Teams

Women's Basketball League (WBL), 1978–1981

Season 1, 1978–1979

Team	# of seasons
Chicago Hustle	2
Dayton Rockettes	1
Houston Angels	2
Iowa Cornets	2
Milwaukee Does	2
Minnesota Fillies	1
New Jersey Gems	2
New York Stars	2

Season 2, 1979–1980

California Dreams	1
Dallas Diamonds	2
New Orleans Pride	2
Philadelphia Fox	less than 1
St. Louis Streak (formerly Dayton Rockettes)	2
San Francisco Pioneers	2
Washington Metros	less than 1

Season 3, 1980–1981

Nebraska Wrangles (formerly California Dreams)	1
New England Gulls	less than 1
Milwaukee Express	0

Women's Basketball Association (WBA), 1993–1995

Season 1, 1993–1994

Team	# of seasons
Illinois Knights	1
Iowa Unicorns	2
Kansas Crusaders	1
Kansas City Mustangs	3
Nebraska Express	3
Oklahoma Cougars	1

Season 2, 1994–1995

Indiana Stars	1
Kansas Marauders	1
Memphis Blues	2
Oklahoma Flames	2
St. Louis River Queens	2

Season 3, 1995–1996

Chicago Twisters	1
Kentucky Marauders	1
Minnesota Stars	1

American Basketball League (ABL), 1996–1999

Season 1, 1996–1997
Atlanta Glory
Colorado Xplosion
Columbus Quest
New England Blizzard
Richmond Rage (later Philadelphia Rage)
Portland Power
San Jose Lasers
Seattle Reign

Season 2, 1997–1998
Long Beach StingRays

Season 3, 1998–1999
Chicago Condors
Nashville Noise

Women's National Basketball Association (WNBA), 1997–

Season 1, 1997
Charlotte Sting
Cleveland Rockers
Houston Comets
New York Liberty
Los Angeles Sparks
Phoenix Mercury
Sacramento Monarchs
Utah Starzz

Season 2, 1998
Detroit Shock
Washington Mystics

Season 3, 1999
Minnesota Lynx
Orlando Miracle

Season 4, 2000
Indiana Fever
Miami Sol
Portland Fire
Seattle Storm

Appendix 2
Hall of Famers

Naismith Memorial Basketball Hall of Fame

Female Inductees

Year	Name	
1984	Senda Berenson Abbott	Contributor
	Bertha F. Teague	Contributor
	L. Margaret Wade	Coach
1992	Nera White	Player
	Lusia Harris Stewart	Player
1993	Ann Meyers	Player
	Uljana Semjonova	Player
1994	Carol Blazejowski	Player
1995	Cheryl Miller	Player
	Anne Donovan	Player
1996	Nancy Lieberman-Cline	Player
1997	Denise Curry	Player
	Joan Crawford	Player
1998	Jody Conradt	Coach
1999	Billie Moore	Coach
2000	Pat Summitt	Coach
2002	Kay Yow	Coach

Women's Basketball Hall of Fame

Class of 1999

Lidia Alexeeva

Senda Berenson Abbott

Carol Blazejowski

Joanne Bracker

Jody Conradt

Joan Crawford

Denise Curry

Anne Donovan

Carol Eckman

Betty Jo Graber

John Head

Nancy Lieberman-Cline

Darlene May

Ann Meyers-Drysdale

Cheryl Miller

Billie Moore

Shin-Ja Park

Harley Redin

Uljana Semjonova

Jim Smiddy

Lusia Harris Stewart

Pat Head Summitt

Bertha Teague

Margaret Wade

Nera White

Class of 2000

Alline Banks Sprouse

Mildred Barnes

Breezy Bishop

E. Wayne Cooley

Nancy Dunkle

Fran Garmon

Dorothy Gaters

Sue Gunter

Rita Horky

Betty Jaynes

George Killian

Kim Mulkey-Robertson

Cindy Noble Hauserman

Lorene Ramsey

Patricia (Trish) Roberts

Sue Rojcewicz

Cathy Rush

Juliene Simpson

Olga Soukharnova

Boris Stankovic

Katherine Washington

Dean Weese

Marcy Weston

Kay Yow

Class of 2001

Van Chancellor

Theresa Grentz

Phyllis Holmes

LaTaunya Pollard

Linda Sharp

C. Vivian Stringer

Vanya Voinova

Hazel Walker

Rosie Walker

Holly Warlick

Class of 2002

Cindy Brogdon

Kamie Ethridge

Margaret Sexton Gleaves

Hortencia de Fatima
    Marcari Oliva

Sandra Meadows

Lea Plarski

Marianne Crawford Stanley

Tara VanDerveer

Appendix 3
Championships

Association for Intercollegiate Athletics for Women (AIAW)

1972 Immaculata, PA
1973 Immaculata, PA
1974 Immaculata, PA
1975 Delta State, MS
1976 Delta State, MS
1977 Delta State, MS
1978 UCLA, CA
1979 Old Dominion, VA
1980 Old Dominion, VA
1981 Louisiana Tech
1982 Rutgers, NJ

National Collegiate Athletic Association (NCAA)

1982 Louisiana Tech
1983 University of Southern California (USC)
1984 USC
1985 Old Dominion, VA
1986 Texas
1987 Tennessee
1988 Louisiana Tech
1989 Tennessee
1990 Stanford, CA
1991 Tennessee
1992 Stanford, CA
1993 Texas Tech
1994 North Carolina
1995 Connecticut
1996 Tennessee
1997 Tennessee
1998 Tennessee
1999 Purdue
2000 Connecticut
2001 Notre Dame
2002 Connecticut

Women's Basketball Olympic Gold Medalists

1976 USSR
1980 USSR
1984 U.S.
1988 U.S.
1992 Unified Team (former USSR)
1996 U.S.
2000 U.S.

Women's National Basketball Association (WNBA)

1997 Houston Comets
1998 Houston Comets
1999 Houston Comets
2000 Houston Comets
2001 Los Angeles Sparks
2002 Los Angeles Sparks

Appendix 4
Awards and Trophies

Naismith Trophy Winners

(Voted for by coaches, sportswriters, and broadcasters.)

1983 Anne Donovan
1984 Cheryl Miller
1985 Cheryl Miller
1986 Cheryl Miller
1987 Clarissa Davis
1988 Sue Wicks
1989 Clarissa Davis
1990 Jennifer Azzi
1991 Dawn Staley
1992 Dawn Staley
1993 Sheryl Swoopes
1994 Lisa Leslie
1995 Rebecca Lobo
1996 Saudia Roundtree
1997 Kate Starbird
1998 Chamique Holdsclaw
1999 Chamique Holdsclaw
2000 Tamika Catchings
2001 Ruth Riley
2002 Sue Bird

Honda Broderick Cup Winners

(Chosen by a panel of college athletic directors. Given to the outstanding woman athlete of the year in an NCAA sport.)

Basketball winners:
1977 Lusia Harris
1978 Ann Meyers
1979 Nancy Lieberman
1984 Cheryl Miller
1986 Kamie Ethridge
1988 Teresa Weatherspoon
1991 Dawn Staley
1995 Rebecca Lobo
1996 Jennifer Rizzotti
1998 Chamique Holdsclaw
2002 Sue Bird

Margaret Wade Trophy Winners

(Voted for by the National Association for Girls and Women in Sports [NAGWS]. Given for academics, community service, and player performance.)

1978 Carol Blazejowski
1979 Nancy Lieberman
1980 Nancy Lieberman
1981 Lynette Woodard
1982 Pam Kelly
1983 LaTaunya Pollard
1984 Janice Lawrence
1985 Cheryl Miller
1986 Kamie Ethridge
1987 Shelly Pennefather
1988 Teresa Weatherspoon
1989 Clarissa Davis
1990 Jennifer Azzi
1991 Daedra Charles
1992 Susan Robinson
1993 Karen Jennings
1994 Carol Ann Shudlick
1995 Rebecca Lobo
1996 Jennifer Rizzotti
1997 DeLisha Milton
1998 Ticha Penicheiro
1999 Stephanie White-McCarty
2000 Edwina Brown
2001 Jackie Stiles
2002 Sue Bird

James E. Sullivan Memorial Award Winners

(James E. Sullivan founded the Amateur Athletic Union [AAU] in 1888. This award is given for character, leadership, sportsmanship, and outstanding athletic achievement in various sports.)

Basketball winners are:

1998   Chamique Holdsclaw
1999   Coco and Kelly Miller

Coach of the Year Award Winners

(Voted for by the WBCA.)

1983   Pat Summitt
1984   Jody Conradt
1985   Jim Foster
1986   Jody Conradt
1987   Theresa Grentz
1988   C. Vivian Stringer
1989   Tara VanDerveer
1990   Kay Yow
1991   Rene Portland
1992   Ferne Labati
1993   C. Vivian Stringer
1994   Marsha Sharp
1995   Pat Summitt
1996   Leon Barmore
1997   Geno Auriemma
1998   Pat Summitt
1999   Carolyn Peck
2000   Geno Auriemma
2001   Muffet McGraw
2002   Geno Auriemma

Carol Eckman Award Winners

(Voted for by the WBCA to a coach whose program brings out sportsmanship, honesty, and integrity in her school and players.)

1986   Laura Mapp
1987   Jody Conradt
1988   Kay Yow
1989   Linda Hill-MacDonald
1990   Maryalyce Jeremiah
1991   Marian Washington
1992   Jill Hutchison
1993   C. Vivian Stringer
1994   Sue Gunter
1995   Ceal Barry
1996   Dr. Joann Rutherford
1997   Amy Ruley
1998   Kay James
1999   Susan Summons
2000   Kathy Delaney-Smith
2001   Juliene B. Simpson
2002   Barbara Stevens

Appendix 5
Historic Rules of the Court

Naismith's Original Rules

January 15, 1892

(edited version)

1. The ball may be thrown in any direction with one or both hands.

2. The ball may be batted in any direction with one or both hands, but never with the fist.

3. A player cannot run with the ball, but must throw it from the spot where he catches it. Allowance is made for a man who catches the ball when running at a good speed.

4. The ball must be held in or between the hands; the arms or the body must not be used for holding the ball.

5. No shouldering, holding, pushing, tripping, or striking of an opponent shall be allowed. The first infringement of this rule by any person shall count as a foul, the second shall disqualify him until the next goal is made. If there is evident intent to injure an opponent (player on the other team) to put him out of the game, no substitute shall be allowed for the disqualified player.

6. A foul is striking at the ball with the fist, violations of Rules 3 and 4, and such violations as are described in Rule 5.

7. If either side makes three consecutive fouls, this shall count as a goal for the opponents. Consecutive means without the opponents in the meantime making a foul.

8. A goal shall be made when the ball is thrown or batted from the ground into the basket and stays there, providing those defending the goal do not touch or disturb the goal. If the ball rests on the edge and the opponent moves the basket, it shall count as a goal.

9. When the ball goes out-of-bounds, it shall be thrown into the field (court) and played by the person first touching it. In case of a dispute, the umpire shall throw it straight into the field. The thrower-in is allowed five seconds. If he holds it longer, it shall go to the opponent. If any side persists in delaying the game, the umpire shall call a foul on them.

10. The umpire shall be the judge of the men and shall note the fouls and notify the referee when three consecutive fouls are made. He has the power to disqualify men according to Rule 5.

11. The referee shall be the judge of the ball and shall decide when the ball is in play, in bounds, to which side it belongs, and shall keep the time. He shall decide when a goal has been made, and keep account of the goals.

12. The time shall be two 15-minute halves, with 5 minutes' rest time between.

13. The side making the most goals in that time shall be declared the winners. In case of a draw (tie), the game may, by agreement of the captains, be continued until another goal is made.

1923 Basketball Training Rules Recommended by the

Department of Hygiene and Physical Educational Board of Athletes Association

(edited version)

Diet: whatever is served at meals except coffee and tea.

No eating between meals except fruit or crackers and milk taken midmorning, midafternoon, or just before going to bed.

Drink eight glasses of milk or water a day besides that taken at meals.

No candy unless in place of dessert.

Sleep in bed every night from 10 P.M. to 6:30 A.M. Rest lying down 15 minutes every day.

Baths: cold bath or shower or spray every morning unless ill effects result. Then consult doctor's office.

Exercise: one-hour active exercise every day that you do not have basketball practice or gymnasium work.

Active exercise may include walking at the rate of 4 miles an hour, skating, snowshoeing, coasting, skiing, running every day. This may be included in your hour's exercise the days that that is taken. These rules hold throughout the basketball season including midyear and apply to everyone playing basketball. It is left to the individual to follow these rules and to report any infringements of them to the upper class captains.

For More Information

Naismith Memorial Basketball Hall of Fame
1150 West Columbus Ave.
Springfield, MA 01101-0179
www.hoophall.com

Women's National Basketball Association
645 5th Ave. Olympic Tower
New York, NY 10022
www.wnba.com

NCAA
6201 College Blvd.
Overland Park, KS 66211-2422
www.ncaa.org

USA Basketball
5465 Mark Dabling Blvd.
Colorado Springs, CO 80918-3842
www.usabasketball.com

Women's Basketball Hall of Fame
900 E. Ave., Suite 390
Knoxville, TN 37915
www.wbhof.com

Youth Basketball of America
PO Box 36108
Orlando, FL 32823
www.yboa.org

Index

Page numbers in *italics* refer to illustrations.

About the Author

Sandra Steen and Susan Steen, former elementary school teachers and librarians, have written several nonfiction books for children. Their picture book, *Car Wash*, was selected as an ALA 2002 Notable.

As teenagers these twins played half-court basketball and were considered to be double trouble. They competed in many sports throughout college. One summer they were pitcher and catcher on a mens' baseball team.

Now living in New Jersey, they like to travel a lot, but not on basketball courts.